A GUIDE TO ORIENTAL CLASSICS

PREPARED AS ONE OF THE COMPANIONS TO ASIAN STUDIES

WM. THEODORE DE BARY, EDITOR

A GUIDE TO

ORIENTAL CLASSICS

SECOND EDITION

PREPARED BY THE STAFF OF THE
ORIENTAL STUDIES PROGRAM
COLUMBIA COLLEGE
AND EDITED BY
WM. THEODORE DE BARY
AND AINSLIE T. EMBREE

COLUMBIA UNIVERSITY PRESS
NEW YORK AND LONDON   1975

The addition of *A Guide to Oriental Classics* to the series "Companions to Asian Studies" was made possible by a grant from the Carnegie Corporation of New York. That Corporation is not, however, the author, owner, publisher, or proprietor of this publication, and is not to be understood as approving by virtue of its grant any of the statements made or views expressed therein.

Copyright © 1964, 1975 Columbia University Press

ISBN: 0–231–03891–7 cloth
ISBN: 0–231–03892–5 paper
Library of Congress Catalog Card Number: 74–14150
Printed in the United States of America

Contributors to the various sections of this Guide are:

NEAR AND MIDDLE EAST: Maan Z. Madina and Jeanette Wakin

INDIA: Ainslie T. Embree, Barbara Miller, Royal Weiler, and Anton Zigmund-Cerbu

BUDDHISM (INDIA, CHINA, AND JAPAN): Jeffrey Broughton, Robert Gimello, and Alex Wayman

CHINA: Wm. Theodore de Bary, C. T. Hsia, and John Meskill

JAPAN: Donald Keene and Royal Tyler

Members of the Oriental Humanities staff and various Teaching Fellows in Oriental Studies have joined the contributors listed above in discussing and refining the materials presented here.

Note on Transliteration

The systems of transliteration used in this Guide are in general those followed in the Introduction to Oriental Civilizations series, edited by Wm. Theodore de Bary, and published by Columbia University Press. No changes have been made, however, in the spelling of book titles or authors' names as they appear in published works.

CONTENTS

INTRODUCTION

INTRODUCTION

This Guide has been compiled as an aid to students and teachers taking up for the first time the major works of Oriental literature and thought. It is designed especially for general education, which emphasizes a careful reading of single whole works and discussion of them in a group. Experience during the past fifteen years in the Columbia College course in the Oriental Humanities has been drawn upon in making the selections and suggesting the discussion topics offered here.

The assumptions of this course, inherited from the parent Humanities course in the Western tradition, have been basically two: that there were certain great works of intellectual and artistic achievement in the Oriental world which any educated person, whatever his own field of specialization, ought to have read; and that these books could be understood and appreciated without prior initiation into the complexities of scholarly research in each field. The first reading, obviously, was not meant to be a final one. The works were classics or "great books" not only in that they deserved to be read by everyone at least once, but also in that, for most persons, they would repay many readings and, for some, endless study. No one thought of this brief introduction as a substitute for more intensive study. The point in Oriental Humanities was to help the nonspecialist appreciate those qualities in a work which made it worth the scholar's lifetime of study, and, moreover, to understand why his own perplexities with certain texts could be resolved only through such exacting research.

Time and experience in teaching the Oriental Humanities have not caused us to abandon these basic assumptions. We learned very early, however, that they would need special

qualification in regard to some Oriental texts. Professor
Trilling, recalling the debate in Columbia College over special
competence versus general intelligence as qualifications for
the Humanities teacher, says that it

> was settled in favor of the party which believed that the purposes of the course
> ... would be adequately served by the general intelligence and enlightenment
> of the teacher. ... The books that would make the substance of the course
> were to be chosen because they were no less pertinent now than when they
> had first been written, and also because their authors were men speaking to
> men, not to certain men who were specially trained to understand them but to
> all men. ... It seemed to us a denial of their nature to suppose that any sort of
> "secondary material" was needed to make them comprehensible.[1]

Accepting this point of view, we nevertheless came to see
that the "general intelligence and enlightenment of the teacher" took for granted, perhaps more than one at first realized,
acquaintance with a common cultural tradition in the West. In
the East this common culture did not exist. We were dealing
with many traditions, not one, and few scholars in Chinese
literature could be presumed also to have read and thought
about important works of the Islamic tradition. Nor had
Muhammad, on the other hand, ever read Confucius. In this
respect, then, Oriental Humanities was not carrying on a
"great conversation" among the great minds of the past, but
rather trying to get a new conversation started.

As regards the teacher, this implied no less need for
"general intelligence and enlightenment," and we have always
been glad when seasoned teachers of the Western Humanities
joined our colloquium (especially since among Western students it would be unnatural and stultifying to exclude from the
conversation their own tradition). But this general intelligence
was most often helpful insofar as it brought specific disciplines

---

[1] Lionel Trilling, preface to *The Proper Study, Essays on Western Classics,*
ed. by Quentin Anderson and Joseph Mazzeo (New York, St. Martin's Press,
1962), p. vi.

to bear on these diverse works, and it functioned most effectively when recourse could be had to the more specialized knowledge of others concerning the subject at hand. The nonspecialist himself, no matter how adventurous and wide-ranging, found it reassuring to have on hand a guide thoroughly familiar with the cultural terrain.

A mixed staff, representing different disciplines and competence in different traditions, provided part of the answer to this situation. Each class section has been conducted by a pair of instructors, one of them acquainted with the language and history of the tradition concerned and the other a knowledgeable outsider. Obviously, however, there are more languages and cultures tributary to the main traditions of Asia than could be represented by a team of teachers, unless either the teachers were to outnumber the students or the students were to be subjected to a kind of Chautauqua series. The classroom instructors or the Colloquium team, therefore, could work best if their individual talents were pooled in a larger staff which met regularly for consultation and which even had the benefit of special lectures by authorities on particularly difficult subjects. (One such subject, perennially, was the *Gathas* of the Avesta, which successive authorities finally convinced us were so obscure and unmanageable as to be poorly suited to this type of course.)

The matter was further complicated by the number of exceptions which our texts provided to the definition of a classic or great book as "addressed to all men." Professor Trilling himself allows that Spinoza was an exception, since he specified that his writing was for a limited group with "strong minds" rather than for the general public. Among Oriental writers there are a few, like Averroes, who would share Spinoza's feeling and make it explicit. There are many more for whom it is implicit. This does not mean that their works, any more than Spinoza's, are lacking in universal appeal or significance. But it does mean that the reader was presumed to have had some prior initiation or preparation for the reading. Especially is this true of certain religious scriptures, and particularly of the traditions arising in India where the esoteric character of religious truth is strongly emphasized and the written text is often considered only an adjunct to personal training and experience under the guidance of a master. In the Far East, Zen texts exemplify the extreme of this type. But this is true not only in religion. The No drama of Japan, in its own way, is quite esoteric, and the effect intended is only to a small degree conveyed by the written text.

In such cases, where the text is an enigma without its context, unless the latter is somehow provided in secondary material, the reader will be forced to make his own conjectures, with results that can rarely be happy. If important works like the *Yoga Sutra* of Patanjali or the *Analects* of Confucius are too often overlaid with commentary, so that their essential meaning is lost in a philological maze, the alternative is not to dispense with commentary altogether. Interpretation and exegesis arise naturally and inevitably from the nature of the text itself.

A careful translation with adequate introduction will normally incorporate as much of this traditional scholarship as is needed to make the text understandable. Readers of the more cryptic Oriental classics, however, soon become aware that there may be several such translations available for certain texts, no one of which can necessarily be canonized as the sole definitive version, while for other texts there may be none which can be considered authoritative. At this point the judgment of experts will be of help to him. Thus something more than a bare reading list has been found desirable for teachers and students in the Oriental Humanities. We could not hold to the principle, as Professor Trilling puts it, ''that there were to be no background lectures or readings, no 'guides', either in textbook or outline form, no 'secondary material' of any kind—all was to be primary.''[2] The teacher, no less than the student, felt a need for precisely such background material or scholarly guidance in areas outside his own immediate competence.

It is out of this realization that the present Guide has been conceived, but conceived in such a way as to reinforce the basic purposes of general education, not to compromise them. Above all, it is a guide which should help to focus the reader's attention on the central issues or essential qualities of a work, relieving the honest mind, insofar as possible, of doubts that these books have something to say to him personally, rather than only to men in some other time or place. Or it may help to avoid misconceptions, perhaps historical, economic, or sociological, which obscure the issues and sometimes blunt the thrust of a writer's point. There are more than enough clichés about the Orient which can be invoked to explain away an uncomfortable idea. How often, for instance, is Buddhism disposed of as simply another manifestation of Indian pessimism, and Indian pessimism as merely an abnormal state of mind reflecting the age-old, extreme poverty of the land

If some such questions of context are diversionary, though nonetheless sincere, the answers to them—or the direction in which to look for answers—may be suggested by a "guide" designed to provide the essential background, without permitting this to preempt the forefront of group discussion. But such a guide can do more than dispose of questions which would otherwise distract the reader or obstruct the discussion. For not all questions of context are ultimately irrelevant, to be refined out of the discussion until we are left alone with some supposedly pure essence of a work in universal terms. If each of these books is a "classic" because there is something eternal and unchanging in it, to which the constant nature of

2 *Ibid.*, p. v.

man responds, each is also unique, the product of a singular intelligence reflecting particular historical circumstances. And it is precisely in their peculiarity that the appeal of many works lies. Reading them becomes an adventure for us when we identify ourselves with the human spirit as it moves through strange surroundings. Similarity and difference illuminate one another, as we come to appreciate the manifold forms and situations in which human sensibility has found expression.

Unfortunately there is no certain criterion, in East or West, by which to judge once and for all which works possess these enduring qualities of greatness. Durability is one obvious test, but the continuing popularity of Shankara with the type of limited audience to which Spinoza appeals may, depending upon the taste of the reader, count for more than the popularity of a Chinese play with generations of common folk. There will always be room for debate over the books which have been put on or kept off our list. This much may be said: over the years it has been a fairly stable list, with the original selections, based largely on the standing of the works in their own tradition, confirmed in at least eight or nine cases out of ten by their perennial success with readers in Oriental Humanities. In the remaining cases there is almost perennial dispute among our staff, and since the addition of a new title can be effected only by the removal of another, the dispute is sure to be intense. Yet even here there is a recurring pattern and a kind of consensus in the end—books stricken from the list in this year's reform are likely to be put forward and reinstated by other reformers a few years hence.

In this Guide we have included somewhat more titles than could be assigned in a given year, providing a range of selection that covers the likely candidates over the years. We have also tried to represent the major genres of literature, thus giving a balanced selection of scriptures, philosophical texts, poetry, drama, and fiction. It should be remembered, however, that these genres were not developed to an equal degree by each of the various Oriental traditions, and we have felt no obligation to include a sample of Indian or Islamic fiction simply because the Chinese and Japanese novel held a prominent place on the list, nor have we hunted for a specimen of epic poetry in China and Japan to place beside the *Mahabharata* or *Ramayana* of India. Our selection aims at representing what has been most valued in these traditions, whatever the form, not at presenting a survey which covers every type of literature, whatever its quality.

One gap, however, is not wholly a matter of choice. Iranian literature is inadequately represented. This revision of the Guide makes an improvement on the earlier one by including the poet Rumi, but severe limitations of time, staff, and suitable translations are still reflected in glaring omissions such as the epic *Shah Namah*.

We realize that not all teachers and students will make the same use of the Guide. Those whose concerns are more religious than literary will perhaps draw more heavily on the Indian readings than upon the Chinese, while those with more literary tastes may bypass Shankara to get at Chinese drama and Japanese *haiku*. There should be enough of both types here for each, given the richness and variety we have to draw upon. What really matters, however, is not whether we have fully satisfied individual tastes, but whether we have included all the basic works which anyone should read.

Clearly, then, this Guide is selective rather than exhaustive. It deals with the most immediate problems of the teacher and student rather than those of the researcher. Our judgment has been exercised upon the translations and secondary works most readily available for use in general education and upon the kind of topic which would best lend itself to group discussion. The topics themselves we have tried to formulate as simply and concisely as possible, for the reason that they are meant to open discussion and not settle it. Their chief value, as we conceive it, is to suggest the essential ideas, issues, or qualities of a work which a reader ought to look for or a satisfactory discussion to touch upon. Granted that interpretations vary, and that some will find much more of significance in a work than others do, still the central questions or features can usually be identified, if only because they are the ones most often in dispute. No speculation or interpretation, however intriguing, should be allowed to take precedence over such basic questions as: what the author is trying to say, what means he chooses to express it, how he defines his problem or his purpose, to what audience he addresses himself, and so forth. Only when these points are clearly understood is it safe to proceed to more general considerations.

For similar reasons the suggested topics do not lean heavily in the direction of comparisons with the Western tradition. It is only natural that such comparisons should be made, since so much of our knowledge is gained or assimilated that way, and one would not seek to avoid in class what arises so spontaneously and irrepressibly in any discussion. Obviously, however, the problem is not to stimulate or suggest comparisons, when so many abound, but rather to keep them within limits. Comparative analysis of several works can be fruitful only if it deals with specific features or concepts in each work for which the grounds of comparability are well established and explicitly defined. Comparisons of whole traditions or religions are almost always out of place and have essentially nothing to do with general education. Indeed, exposure to the complexities of different cultural traditions and religious systems should make the student increasingly conscious that such questions, while not insignificant, require a depth of scholarly study and fullness of treatment quite beyond an introductory course. It is not upon their solution that the value of such a course depends, but upon appreciation of the books in and for themselves.

WM. THEODORE DE BARY

I. Classics of the Islamic Tradition

GENERAL WORKS

Basic Bibliographies and Reference Works

The Encyclopaedia of Islam, New Edition. 3 vols. and continuing. Leiden, E. J. Brill, 1954—
Contains the most recent authoritative articles in all fields of Islamic studies. Gradually replacing the *First Edition*, 4 vols. and *Supplement*, Leiden, E. J. Brill, 1913-38.
Jean Sauvaget's Introduction to the History of the Muslim East, A Bibliographical Guide. Recast by Claude Cahen. Berkeley, University of California Press, 1965.
A valuable annotated guide.
Pearson, J. D. *Index Islamicus, 1906-1955,* with three *Supplements, 1956-1960, 1961-1965,* and 1966-1970. Cambridge, Heffer, 1958-72.
A classified and exhaustive list of articles dealing with Islamic subjects.

Islamic Literature

Arberry, A. J. *Aspects of Islamic Civilization as Depicted in the Original Texts.* London, Allen and Unwin, 1964; paperback ed. University of Michigan Press (Ann Arbor Paperback), 1967.
An anthology with commentary.
Browne, E. G. *A Literary History of Persia.* 4 vols. Cambridge University Press, 1928-30; repr. 1956-59.
A detailed account that includes many translations and material on Persian history in general.
Gibb, H. A. R. *Arabic Literature: An Introduction.* London, Oxford University Press, 1926; 2d rev. ed. Oxford, Clarendon Press, 1963.

Excellent survey of all varieties of Arabic writings up to the eighteenth century. Includes a selected bibliography of literature in translation.

Kritzeck, J. *Anthology of Islamic Literature.* New York, Holt, Rinehart and Winston, 1964; paperback ed. New York, New American Library (Mentor), 1966.
Short selections from Islamic literature to 1800.

Levy, Reuben. *An Introduction to Persian Literature.* New York, Columbia University Press, 1969.
A useful short survey.

Nicholson, R. A. *A Literary History of the Arabs.* 2d ed. Cambridge University Press, 1930; paperback ed. 1969.
A standard work, well informed and richly documented.

Rypka, Jan. *History of Iranian Literature.* Dordrecht, D. Reidel, 1968.
A comprehensive work.

Schroeder, Eric. *Muhammad's People.* Portland, Maine, Wheelwright, 1955.
A selection of Islamic writings on a variety of subjects, artfully translated.

Trabulsi, Amjad. *La Critique poétique des Arabes jusqu' au V° siècle de l'Hégire.* Damascus, Institut français de Damas, 1955.
An excellent account of Arabic literary theory and literary criticism.

ISLAMIC RELIGION AND PHILOSOPHY

Arberry, A. J. *Revelation and Reason in Islam.* London, Allen and Unwin, 1957; New York, Macmillan, 1957.
Readable discussion of the conflict between reason and revelation and its solution in Islam.

De Boer, T. J. *The History of Philosophy in Islam,* tr. by Edward R. Jones. London, Luzac, 1903; paperback ed. New York, Dover, 1967.

While much new research has been done, this older account still provides a useful framework.

Gibb, H. A. R. *Mohammedanism: An Historical Survey.* 2d ed. London, Oxford University Press, 1953; paperback eds. New York, New American Library (Mentor), 1955; and New York, Harper (Galaxy), 1962.

A brief, graceful survey by a distinguished authority.

Gibb, H. A. R. and J. H. Kramers, eds. *Shorter Encyclopaedia of Islam.* Leiden, E. J. Brill, 1953; Ithaca, Cornell University Press, 1953.

A collection of articles on religion and law from the first edition of *The Encyclopaedia of Islam.*

Guillaume, Alfred. *Islam.* Harmondsworth, Penguin Books, 1954.

A background study that expertly examines the great religious doctrines and practices in historical context.

———— "Philosophy and Theology," in Sir T. Arnold and A. Guillaume, eds. *The Legacy of Islam.* Oxford, Clarendon Press, 1931; repr. 1952; pp. 239-83.

An excellent brief account of the influence of Islamic thought on Europe and its transmission through Spain.

Jeffery, Arthur. *A Reader on Islam.* The Hague, Mouton, 1962.

Valuable collection of translations from Arabic writings, with notes, illustrating Islamic beliefs and practices.

Lerner, Ralph, and Muhsin Mahdi, eds. *Medieval Political Philosophy: A Sourcebook.* Glencoe, Ill., Free Press, 1963.

Part I gives selections from Islamic philosophy.

MacDonald, Duncan B. *Development of Muslim Theology, Jurisprudence, and Constitutional Theory.* New York, Scribner's, 1903; repr. Beirut, Khayat's, 1965.

Sound, old-fashioned treatment.

Watt, W. Montgomery. *Islamic Philosophy and Theology.* Edinburgh University Press, 1962.

A clear, concise account with excellent bibliographies.

Walzer, Richard. *Greek into Arabic: Essays on Islamic Philosophy.* Oxford, Cassirer, 1962; Los Angeles, University of Southern California Press, 1969.
Contains some important articles, but see especially an excellent summary on pp. 1-28.

ISLAMIC HISTORY

Arnold, T. W., and Alfred Guillaume, eds. *The Legacy of Islam.* Oxford, Clarendon Press, 1931.
Contains many authoritative articles on Islamic religious thought, science, and art, and their influence upon Europe.
Gibb, H. A. R. *Studies on the Civilization of Islam,* ed. by S. J. Shaw and J. R. Polk. Boston, Beacon Press, 1962; paperback ed. 1968.
Articles on the history and culture of Islam.
Hitti, Philip K. *History of the Arabs, from the Earliest Times to the Present.* 8th ed. London, Macmillan, 1963; paperback ed. New York, St. Martin's Press, 1963.
A standard work.
Levy, Reuben. *The Social Structure of Islam.* Cambridge University Press, 1957; paperback ed. 1962.
A general discussion of Islamic institutions.
Lewis, Bernard. *The Arabs in History.* 4th ed. (revised). London, Hutchinson, 1966; paperback ed. New York, Harper (Torchbook), 1967.
Excellent historical survey.
Von Grunebaum, G. E. *Medieval Islam: A Study in Cultural Orientation.* 2d ed. Chicago, University of Chicago Press, 1953; paperback ed. Chicago (Phoenix), 1961.
A rich general view of Muslim culture and its prevailing conceptions.
————, ed. *Unity and Variety in Muslim Civilization.* Chicago, University of Chicago Press, 1955.
A collection of essays on Islamic literature, history, and institutions.

THE SEVEN ODES
(AL-MUʿALLAQĀT)

This collection, the most celebrated among several, has exerted a lasting influence on Islamic poetry. It is traditionally assigned to the sixth century A.D.

TRANSLATIONS

a. COMPLETE

Arberry, A. J. *The Seven Odes.* London, Allen and Unwin, 1957; New York, Macmillan, 1957.
A vigorous yet sensitive prose rendering which tends to follow in simple, clear English the rhythm of the original. Introductions are mainly concerned with the history of translation.

Blunt, Anne, and Wilfred S. Blunt. *The Seven Golden Odes of Pagan Arabia, Known Also as The Moallakat.* London, the Translators, 1903. (Tr. from the original Arabic by Lady Anne Blunt; done into English verse by Wilfred S. Blunt.)
A verse translation in archaistic English which takes as a model FitzGerald's very freehanded method of rendering the *Rubā ʿīyāt.*

Jones, William. *The Moallakát or Seven Arabian Poems, Which Were Suspended on the Temple at Mecca.* London, 1783. Also available in Sir William Jones, *Works* (London, 1799), IV, 245-335.
The pioneer translation in Latinized English prose.

Wolff, Philipp. *Muallakat, die Sieben Preisgedichte der Araber.* Rotweil, 1857.
A metrical translation by a competent translator.

b. SELECTIONS

Lyall, C. J. *Translations of Ancient Arabian Poetry, Chiefly Prae-Islamic.* London, Williams and Norgate, 1930; New York, Columbia University Press, 1930.
Verse translations of an excellent collection chiefly from ancient Arabian poetry, which attempt to imitate the original meters, with a useful introduction and notes.

Nicholson, R. A. *Translations of Eastern Poetry and Prose.* Cambridge University Press, 1922; pp. 1-27.
The first twenty-five selections are translations of short passages from ancient Arabian poetry ranging from a free to a more literal rendering.

Rückert, Friedrich. *Hamāsa, oder die ältesten arabischen Volkslieder, einsammelt von Abu Temmam, übersetzt und erläutert.* 2 vols. Stuttgart, Liesching, 1846.
Excellent verse translations of ancient Arabian poetry.

SECONDARY READINGS

Blachère, Régis. *Histoire de la littérature arabe.* 3 vols. Paris, Maisonneuve, 1952-66.
The first two volumes constitute the best account of pre-Islamic and early Islamic literature.

Encyclopaedia of Islam, New Edition. Articles " ͨArabiyya" (Arabic Language and Literature; I, pp. 561-603, especially pp. 583-86); "(Djazirat) al- ͨArab" (Arabian Peninsula; I, pp. 533-56); "Badw" (Nomad; I, pp. 872-92).
Also see articles under names of individual poets.

Gabrieli, Francesco. "Ancient Arabic Poetry," *Diogenes*, no. 40 (Winter, 1962), pp. 82-95.

Gibb, H. A. R. *Arabic Literature.* 2d rev. ed. Oxford, Clarendon Press, 1963; pp. 1-31.

Hitti, Philip K. *History of the Arabs, from the Earliest Times to the Present.* 8th ed. London, Macmillan, 1963; paperback ed. New York, St. Martin's Press, 1963.

Chapters 1, 2, 3 (especially chapter 3).

Nicholson, R. A. *A Literary History of the Arabs.* 2d ed. Cambridge University Press, 1930; paperback ed. 1969.

Chapters 1, 2, 3 (especially chapter 3).

Von Grunebaum, G. E. "Arabic Poetics," in H. Franz and G. L. Anderson, eds., *Indiana University Conference on Oriental-Western Literary Relations.* Chapel Hill, University of North Carolina Press, 1955; pp. 27-46. Also available in a separate reprint.

TOPICS FOR DISCUSSION

1. The special place of Arabian poetry: the Arab love of poetry; the poet and his role in pre-Islamic society; poetry as a model of literary excellence, as a record of the past, and as a mirror of Bedouin life.

2. The natural setting: desert background and pastoral life; the Arab's feeling for nature as shown through concrete, sensuous imagery and use of local color.

3. The Bedouin spirit: nomadic love of freedom and independence; chivalry, generosity, and tribal loyalty as dominant ideals.

4. Arab paganism and hedonism; underlying pessimism and signs of a religious awakening.

5. Intense subjectivity of the poet; his personal experience always central.

6. Structure and style: metrical complexity and elaborateness; the highly conventionalized nature of the odes (stereotyped beginning, common themes, epithets, figures of speech); casual mood and spontaneity of expression; lack of unified theme.

7. Special qualities of individual poets:
   a. Imr al-Qais: his love adventures, daring, feeling for nature.

b. Ṭarafa: his passionate tone, hedonism.
c. Zuhair: moral earnestness and depth of religious feeling.
d. Labīd: his feeling for the desert, pessimism.
e. 'Antara: heroism and chivalry.
f. 'Amr: glorification of self, family, and tribe.
g. Ḥārith ibn Ḥilliza: panegyric; conception of justice.

THE KORAN (AL-QUR'ĀN)

The revelations to the Prophet Muhammad accepted by Muslims as God's final word. Compiled ca. 651.

TRANSLATIONS

a. COMPLETE

Arberry, A. J. *The Koran Interpreted.* 2 vols. London, Allen and Unwin, 1955; New York, Macmillan, 1955.

An attempt to popularize the *Koran* and to do justice to the rhetoric and artistry of the original text; though marred by its tendency to archaize and to break the original verses into short lines, of all the translations into English it is recommended for general extended reading.

Bell, Richard. *The Qur'ān, Translated, with a Critical Rearrangement of the Surahs.* 2 vols. Edinburgh, Clark, 1937-39.

The best scholarly translation available in English and the first serious attempt at a critical evaluation and rearrangement of the contents of each *sura*; especially recommended for brief, exact quotations and for more specialized uses.

Blachère, Régis. *Le Coran.* 3 vols. Paris, Maisonneuve, 1949-51.

A distinguished scholarly translation that attempts to reconstruct the probable chronological order of the verses. With notes and a detailed subject index; Vol. I is an introduction.

Palmer, Edward H. *The Qur'an.* (Sacred Books of the East, vols. 6, 9.) Oxford, Clarendon Press, 1880.

Also available under the title *The Koran,* with an introduction by R. A. Nicholson. Oxford University Press, 1928; reissued in World's Classics ed.

An early translation; rather literal but deserving of mention.

Pickthall, M. M. *The Meaning of the Glorious Koran: An Explanatory Translation.* London, Knopf, 1930; New York,

Knopf, 1931; New York, New American Library (Mentor), 1953.

An artistic and sensitive rendering by an English Muslim convert; valuable for presenting the modern orthodox interpretation of the teachings of the *Koran.*

Rodwell, J. M. *The Koran.* London, 1861. Rev. ed. (Everyman's Library), London, Dent, 1953; New York, Dutton, 1953 (reissue of 1909 ed.)

A literal version rendered in a biblical style of English which has the *suras* arranged in roughly chronological order, with useful short footnotes; recommended for general teaching purposes.

Sale, George. *The Koran with Notes and a Preliminary Discourse.* London, 1734 (new eds., 1825, 1857, 1878); Philadelphia, 1870. Reprinted with introduction by Sir Edward Dennison Ross. London, F. Warne, 1921.

An early and literal rendering valuable for its attempt to adhere to the traditional orthodox interpretation.

b. SELECTIONS

Arberry, A. J. *The Holy Koran: An Introduction with Selections.* London, Allen and Unwin (Ethical and Religious Classics of East and West, no. 9), 1953; New York, Macmillan, 1953.

Short Koranic selections freely rendered; designed for the general reader.

Jeffery, Arthur. *The Koran: Selected Suras.* New York, Heritage Press, 1958.

An excellent, scholarly selection with useful introduction and notes.

Schroeder, Eric. *Muhammad's People.* Portland, Maine, Wheelwright, 1955; pp. 24-144.

Short selections, interspersed with traditions relating the passages to episodes in the life of Muhammad. A sensitive, if somewhat free, translation.

SECONDARY READINGS

Andrae, Tor. *Mohammed, the Man and His Faith*, tr. from the German by T. Menzel. London, Allen and Unwin, 1956; New York, Barnes and Noble, 1957.

Bell, Richard. *Introduction to the Qur'ān*. Edinburgh, Edinburgh University Press, 1953; rev. ed. Chicago, Aldine, 1958.
The best short introduction in English.

Blachère, R. *Introduction au Coran*. Paris, Maisonneuve, 1959.

Ibn Hisham, 'Abd al-malik. *The Life of Muhammad: A Translation of Ishāq's Sīrat rasūl Allah*, tr. by Alfred Guillaume. Oxford University Press, 1955.
An early biography of the Prophet Muhammad, reconstructed in a scholarly translation.

Jeffery, Arthur. "The Qur'ān," in Wm. Theodore de Bary, ed., *Approaches to the Oriental Classics*. New York, Columbia University Press, 1959; pp. 49-61.

Stanton, H. U. Weitbrecht. *The Teaching of the Qur'ān: with an Account of Its Growth and a Subject Index*. London, Central Board of Missions and SPCK, 1919; New York, Macmillan, 1919.
Contains a valuable subject index.

Von Grunebaum, G. E. *Islam: Essays in the Nature and Growth of a Cultural Tradition*. London, Routledge and Kegan Paul, 1955. Chapter 4, pp. 80-95.

Watt, W. Montgomery. *Companion to the Qur'ān*. London, Allen and Unwin, 1967.
A commentary intended for the general reader, prepared for use with Arberry's translation.

——*Muhammad at Mecca*. Oxford, Clarendon Press, 1953.

——*Muhammad at Medina*. Oxford, Clarendon Press, 1956.

——*Muhammad, Prophet and Statesman*. London, Oxford University Press, 1961; paperback ed. 1964.

Like the same author's other two works on Muhammad, of which this is an abridgement, an attempt to understand the Prophet's activity within his own social and economic environment.

TOPICS FOR DISCUSSION

1. The *Koran* as a book.
    a. Muhammad as Prophet and the *Koran* as scripture.
    b. The *Koran* as literature: form and style.
    c. In what sense is it original or distinctive?
    d. The question of chronology.
2. The unity and transcendence of Allah as the central conception of the *Koran*.
    a. His majestic aloofness in contrast to his tender compassion.
    b. His absolute freedom as against his involvement in a moralistic system which insures retribution or reward for every action.
3. Man's relation to God.
    a. Man face to face with God; absence of a mediator.
    b. Fear *(wara')* as the essential element of faith and basis of piety (*taqwā*).
    c. Man's unconditional allegiance to Allah: Islam as submission to Allah's will.
    d. Equality of all men in their creaturely relation to God.
    e. Man's nature: created good but weak and prone to sin.
4. Salvation.
    a. Subjectively through piety; objectively through submission to Allah's will.
    b. Predestination.
    c. The torments of hell and delights of paradise.
5. The *Koran* as the basis of the social order.
    a. Life in this world as a means to salvation in the next.
    b. Emphasis upon "works and obedience."

c. The *Koran* as the source of all law.
6. The relation of Islam to Judaism and Christianity: "The People of the Book."

THE RING OF THE DOVE (ṬAWQ AL-ḤAMĀMA), BY IBN ḤAZM (994–1064)

A book on the theory of love, by an Andalusian Muslim scholar.

TRANSLATIONS

Arberry, A. J. *The Ring of the Dove, a Treatise on the Art and Practice of Arab Love.* London, Luzac, 1953.
A superior translation that conveys the spirit of the original.
Bercher, Léon. *Le Collier du Pigeon ou de l'Amour et des Amants.* Algiers, Editions Carbonels, 1949.
Gabrieli, Francesco. *Il Collare della Colomba, sull'amore e gli amanti.* Bari, Giuseppe Laterza e Gigli, 1949.
García Gómez, E. *El Collar de la Paloma.* Madrid, La Sociedad de Estudios y Publicaciones, 1952.
Contains an appendix devoted to works on the *Ṭawq.*
Nykl, A. R. *A Book Containing the Risāla Known as the Dove's Neck-Ring about Love and Lovers.* Paris, Paul Geuthner, 1931.
A pioneer effort, although the translation is somewhat awkward. The important introduction discusses the relationship between the Arabic work and the writings of the Troubadors.
Weisweiler, Max. *Halsband der Taube, über die Liebe und die Liebenden.* Leiden, E. J. Brill, 1944.

SECONDARY READINGS

Abel, Armand. "Spain: Internal Division," in *Unity and Variety in Muslim Civilization,* ed. by G. E. von Grune-

baum, University of Chicago Press, 1956, pp. 207-30.
Contains an interesting interpretation of Ibn Ḥazm's *Ṭawq al-Ḥamāma.*

Arberry, A. J. *Moorish Poetry.* Cambridge, Cambridge University Press, 1953.
An English translation of an anthology compiled by Ibn Saʿīd in 1243, called *The Pennants.* Parts of the Arabic work were translated by E. García Gómez, *Poemas arábigoandaluces,* Madrid, 1930 and 1943.

Encyclopaedia of Islam, New Edition. Articles "Ibn Ḥazm" (III, pp. 790-99); "al-Andalus" (I, pp. 486-503); and " ʿArabiyya" (I, pp. 599-603; appendix: Arabic literature in Spain).

Gibb, H. A. R. *Arabic Literature: An Introduction.* 2d rev. ed. Oxford, Clarendon Press, 1963.
Chapter 5, pp. 108-16; chapter 6, pp. 136-40; chapter 7, pp. 149-55. See the bibliography for related works in translation.

Hitti, Philip K. *History of the Arabs, from the Earliest Times to the Present.* 8th ed. London, Macmillan, 1963; paperback ed. New York, St. Martin's Press, 1963.
See Part IV, "The Arabs in Europe: Spain and Sicily," pp. 493-615.

Nykl, A. R. *Hispano-Arabic Poetry and its Relations with the Old Provençal Troubadors.* Baltimore, J. H. Furst, 1946.
A survey of Andalusian poetry with information on poets and translations of selected passages.

Watt, W. Montgomery and Pierre Cachia. *A History of Islamic Spain* ("Islamic Surveys, IV"). Edinburgh, Edinburgh University Press, 1965; paperback ed. New York, Doubleday (Anchor), 1967.
An excellent short survey, with useful bibliography, covering the period from 711 to 1492. Special sections deal with poetry and prose literature.

TOPICS FOR DISCUSSION

1. Ibn Ḥazm as a psychologist and observer of the human

scene. Use of examples drawn from personal experience. Is the *Tawq* a work of entertainment, a strictly literary work, or does it have another purpose? The author's preoccupation with language and the apparent and hidden meanings of words. Its value as a reflection of life and manners in 11th century Cordova.

2. Ibn Ḥazm's moral and ethical views. The increasing seriousness of the work and the significance of the last chapters. Hints of pessimism and bitterness. The standards of conduct portrayed; do they conform to or oppose those considered proper in the orthodox Muslim world?

3. Techniques and organization of the work. Systematic treatment of the material: the various categories of love; nature and essence of love; causes, symptoms and effects; the tragedies of love.

4. The significance of the work in relation to European troubador poetry and ideas of courtly love. The themes of the martyrs of love and chaste love. Ibn Ḥazm's theory of profane love.

5. Relationship between profane love and the divine love of the Muslim martyrs. Is there an anti-ascetic and anti-mystical trend in the *Tawq*?

THE ASSEMBLIES OF AL-ḤARĪRĪ (MAQĀMĀT AL-ḤARĪRĪ) (1054–1122)

Fifty episodes reflecting the mores of the times and the Arab love of linguistic dexterity.

TRANSLATIONS

a. COMPLETE

Chenery, Thomas, and F. Steingass. *The Assemblies of al-Ḥarīrī.* (Oriental Translation Fund, New Series, III, 1867; IX [reissue of vol. I] and X [vol. II], 1898.) 2 vols. London, Williams, 1867-98. Repr. 1969. Vol. I tr. by Chenery; vol. II tr. by Steingass.
An excellent literal rendering in prose, with a lengthy introduction and notes.

b. SELECTIONS

Nicholson, Reynold A. *Translations of Eastern Poetry and Prose.* Cambridge University Press, 1922. Selections 112, 113.
A strict literal translation in rhymed prose of two assemblies (nos. 11 and 12), which keeps to the original form.
Preston, Theodore. *"Makāmāt" or Rhetorical Anecdotes of Al-Ḥarīrī of Basra.* London, 1850.
A free translation of twenty assemblies rendered in a mixture of prose and verse, together with notes and a summary of the untranslated assemblies.
Rückert, Friedrich. *Die Verwandlungen des Abū Seid von Serūg, oder die Makamen des Hariri.* 2d ed. Stuttgart and Tübingen, 1837.

A skillful imitation in verse of the composition of the original; too free to be considered an accurate translation.

SECONDARY READINGS

Blachère, R., and P. Masnou. *Choix de maqāmāt, traduites de l'arabe avec une étude sur le genre.* Paris, Klincksieck, 1957. A translation of fifteen assemblies by an earlier author, al-Hamadhānī. Contains a valuable introductory essay on the genre.

Encyclopaedia of Islam, New Edition. Articles "al-Harīrī" (III, pp. 221-22); and "al-Hamadhānī" (III, pp. 106-7).

Nicholson, Reynold A. *A Literary History of the Arabs.* 2d ed. Cambridge, Cambridge University Press, 1930; paperback ed. 1969. Chapter 7, especially pp. 328-36.

Prendergast, W. J. *The Maqāmāt of Badī' al-Zamān al-Hamadhānī.* London, Luzac, 1915. Another work in the same literary genre as that of Al-Harīrī.

Von Grunebaum, G. E. *Islam: Essays in the Nature and Growth of a Cultural Tradition.* London, Routledge and Kegan Paul, 1955. Chapter 5, pp. 95-110: "The Spirit of Islam as Shown in Its Literature," especially pp. 104-9.

——— *Medieval Islam: A Study in Cultural Orientation.* 2d ed. Chicago, University of Chicago Press, 1953; paperback ed. (Phoenix), 1961. Chapter 8, pp. 258-93: "Self-Expression: Literature and History."

TOPICS FOR DISCUSSION

1. The *Assemblies* as a literary form.
   a. The alternation of rhymed prose and poetry in each assembly, and its function.
   b. Quick transition from one subject to another and from seriousness to jest.

    c. No concern with maintaining the unity of the original or principal theme of the *Assemblies* as a whole. Episodic character of the work; lack of sustained narrative development.

    d. Combination of thematic simplicity with linguistic and literary complexity.

    e. Use of stereotyped characters and situations as vehicles for the display of literary technique and linguistic virtuosity.

    f. The *maqāma* in Muslim Spain as a possible inspiration for the picaresque novel of the sixteenth century.

2. The *Assemblies* as expressions of the Islamic spirit.

    a. Repetition of characteristic Islamic themes and images: the mosque, pilgrimage, graveyard, etc.

    b. Use of the *Assemblies* for the exposition of Muslim doctrine: the relation of entertainment to instruction; Al-Ḥarīrī's claim to be one "who composes stories for instruction, not for display," and "who assents to doctrine and 'guides to the right path.'"

    c. Koranic verses and imagery, and the relating of *Ḥadīth* (traditions concerning the Prophet).

    d. Pervasiveness of the religious spirit in general.

3. The *Assemblies* as an expression of the Arab love of eloquence and scholarship.

4. The *Assemblies* as true pictures of the life and culture of medieval Islam.

5. Abū Zayd as the central figure of the *Assemblies*; Abū Zayd as hero and Al-Ḥārith as his foil.

THE THOUSAND AND ONE NIGHTS (ALF LAYLA WA-LAYLA)

Folk literature composed and added to between the tenth and sixteenth centuries.

TRANSLATIONS

a. COMPLETE

Burton, Richard F. *The Arabian Nights' Entertainments, or, The Book of a Thousand Nights and a Night.* 16 vols. Benares, 1885-88. Besides the Smithers edition in 12 vols. (London, 1894-97) and Lady Burton's edition in 6 vols. (London, 1886), there were several complete reprints of this translation, including those of the Limited Editions Club (6 vols., 1934) and the Heritage Press (6 vols. in 3, 1956).
A literal translation rendered in a mixture of archaic and slang expressions, attempting to reproduce the oriental flavor of the original. The work borrows extensively from Payne's translation.

Littmann, E. *Die Erzählungen aus den Tausendundein Nächten,* zum ersten Mal nach dem arabischen Urtext der Calcuttaer Ausgabe aus dem Jahre 1839 übertragen. 6 vols. Leipzig, 1923-28; repr. Wiesbaden, Insel-Verlag, 1954.
A distinguished translation by one of the leading scholars of the *Nights.* Conveys the proper tone and character of the original.

Payne, John. *The Book of the Thousand Nights and One Night.* 9 vols. London, 1882-84; 4 supplementary vols., 1884-88. There have been several complete reprints.
The first complete translation in English, noted for its strict literal rendering of the original. It suffers from the lack of

explanatory notes and from the use of obscure slang expressions.

b. SELECTIONS

Arberry, A. J. *Scheherezade: Tales from the Thousand and One Nights.* London, Allen and Unwin, 1953; New York, New American Library (Mentor), 1955.
A lively, up-to-date, free rendering in modern colloquial language of four well-known and representative tales.

Campbell, Joseph, ed. *The Portable Arabian Nights.* New York, Viking Press, 1952.
Selections from Payne's translation with a summary of all the plots. The edition is marred by a poor introduction.

Dawood, N. J. *The Thousand and One Nights: The Hunchback, Sindbad and Other Tales.* Harmondsworth, Penguin Books, 1954.
—— *Aladdin and Other Tales from the 1001 Nights.* Harmondsworth, Penguin Books, 1957.
Selections in modern prose.

Lane, Edward W. *The Thousand and One Nights: The Arabian Nights' Entertainment.* 3 vols. London, C. Knight, 1839-41; 2d ed., 1847. New ed., ed. by E. S. Poole, 3 vols. London, Bickers, 1877.
The earliest important translation, rendered into archaic English. Though incomplete and literal, it is valuable for its accuracy and its extensive commentary.

Torrens, Henry. *The Book of the Thousand Nights and One Night.* London, W. H. Allen, 1838; Calcutta, W. Thacker, 1838.
A literal translation of 51 tales noted for its attempt to emphasize the literary value of the *Nights.*

SECONDARY READINGS

Elisséeff, Nikita. *Thèmes et Motifs des Mille et Une Nuits; Essai de Classification.* Beyrouth, Imprimerie Catholique,

1949.

Contains an extensive bibliography.

Encyclopaedia of Islam, New Edition. Article "Alf Layla wa-Layla" (I, pp. 358-64).

Gerhardt, Mia I. *The Art of Story-Telling.* Leiden, E. J. Brill, 1963.

The best comprehensive literary study of the *Nights.*

Horovitz, J. "The Origins of the Arabian Nights," tr. from the German. *Islamic Culture,* I (1927), 36-57.

Lane, Edward W. *Arabian Society in the Middle Ages: Studies from The Thousand and One Nights,* ed. by Stanley Lane-Poole. London, Chatto and Windus, 1883.

Von Grunebaum, G. E. *Medieval Islam: A Study in Cultural Orientation.* 2d ed. Chicago, University of Chicago Press, 1953; paperback ed. (Phoenix), 1961.

Chapter 9, pp. 294-319: "Creative Borrowing: Greece in the *Arabian Nights.*"

TOPICS FOR DISCUSSION

1. Origin and authorship; the *Nights* as a product of the popular imagination.
2. The *Nights* as an example of the storytelling art; the framestory and the question of structural unity.
3. The *Nights* as a vivid expression of the mood and temper of medieval Islam and a portrayal of its way of life.
4. The supernatural element; the role of magic and *jinn* in the *Nights* as compared to the *Koran.*
5. Religion as expressed in the form and spirit of the *Nights.*
6. The morality of the *Nights.* Is there any consistent ethical viewpoint?
7. The concept of the hero: whether the *Nights* are stories of character, accident, or fate; character analysis of Judar, Aladdin, etc.
8. Love and the pursuit of pleasure.
9. The impact of the *Nights* on the West and the reasons for its popularity.

DELIVERANCE FROM ERROR (AL-MUNQIDH MIN AL-ḌALĀL), BY AL-GHAZĀLĪ (1058–1111)

The spiritual autobiography of one of Islam's most influential thinkers.

TRANSLATIONS

Field, Claud H. A. *The Confessions of Al Ghazzali.* (Wisdom of the East series.) London, John Murray, 1909; reprinted under title *The Alchemy of Happiness*, 1910.
This first translation into English is in a very free style. Although quite readable, it contains several errors in translation and lacks scholarly precision in the rendering of technical terms.

Jabre, Farid. *Al-Munqidh min Aḍalāl (Erreur et Délivrance).* (Collection UNESCO d'Oeuvres représentatives) Commission internationale pour la Traduction des Chefs-d'oeuvre, Beirut, 1959.
An excellent translation with an extensive introduction and useful notes.

Watt, W. M. *The Faith and Practice of Al-Ghazālī.* London, Allen and Unwin, 1953.
A somewhat literal rendering of Ghazālī's *Al-Munqidh* and the *Bidāya;* a good translation, sensitive and reliable.

SECONDARY READINGS

Arberry, A. J. *Sufism, an Account of the Mystics of Islam.* London, Allen and Unwin, 1950.

Encylopaedia of Islam, New Edition. Article "al-Ghazālī" (II, pp. 1038-41).

Faris, Nabih Amin. *The Book of Knowledge, Being the Translation of the Kitāb al-'Ilm.* Lahore, Ashraf, 1962. The first sections of al-Ghazālī's great *summa theologica,* the *Revival of the Religious Sciences.*

Gairdner, W. H. T. *Al-Ghazzālī's Mishkāt al-Anwār (The Niche for Lights).* London, Royal Asiatic Society, 1924; repr. Lahore, Ashraf, 1952.

MacDonald, D. B. "The Life of Al Ghazālī," *Journal of the American Oriental Society,* XX (1899), 122-29.

Nicholson, R. A. *The Idea of Personality in Sufism.* Cambridge University Press, 1923; repr. Lahore, Ashraf, 1964.

———— *The Mystics of Islam.* (The Quest series.) London, G. Bell, 1914; repr. London, Routledge and Kegan Paul, 1966.

———— *Studies in Islamic Mysticism.* Cambridge University Press, 1921.

Sabbagh, Toufic. *Lettre au Disciple (Ayyuhā 'l-Walad).* (Collection UNESCO d'Oeuvres représentatives) Commission internationale pour la Traduction des Chefs-d'oeuvre, Beirut, 1959.
A translation of a short popular work by al-Ghazālī on the mystic's life.

Smith, Margaret. *Al-Ghazālī, the Mystic.* London, Luzac, 1944.

Von Grunebaum, G. E. *Medieval Islam.* Chicago, University of Chicago Press, 1946.
Chapter 4, "The Religious Foundations: Piety," pp. 108-17, 124-33; chapter 8, "Self-Expression: Literature and History," especially pp. 270-75.

Watt, W. Montgomery. *Muslim Intellectual: A study of Al-Ghazali.* Edinburgh University Press, 1963.

Wensinck, A. J. *On the Relation Between Al-Ghazālī's Cosmology and His Mysticism.* Amsterdam, Noord-Hollandsche uitgevers-maatschappij, 1933.

———— *La pensée de Ghazali.* Paris, Adrien-Maisonneuve, 1940.

TOPICS FOR DISCUSSION

1. Ghazālī's informal and engaging style; his clarity of presentation; his wide resources and knowledge; his power of illustration and extensive use of imagery.
2. *Al-Munqidh* as an autobiographical work; normative rather than descriptive in nature; development and sequence of stages; characterization of contemporaries; its scholastic style.
3. Ghazālī's primary concern: how to achieve certainty concerning ultimate religious truths (*awwalīyāt*).
4. Ghazālī's evaluation of sense perception, intellect, and faith based on "blind acceptance" (*taqlīd*) as sources of "certain" knowledge (*yaqīn*).
5. The various approaches to knowledge, namely, philosophy, theology, "authoritative instruction" (*ta 'līm*), and mysticism. The place of the philosophic and mathematical sciences in relation to the religious sciences. The general usefulness of these approaches; their ability to achieve certain knowledge of ultimate religious truths. Mystic intuitive knowledge (*kashf*) as the only means of achieving such certainty.
6. The reconciliation of mysticism and revealed tradition.
7. The nature of the religious experience and its practical effect on the conduct of life.

ON THE HARMONY OF RELIGION AND PHILOSOPHY (KITĀB FAṢL AL-MAQĀL), BY AVERROES (IBN RUSHD) (1126–98)

A classic attempt to reconcile religion and philosophy.

TRANSLATIONS

Gauthier, Leon. *Traité décisif (Façl al-maqāl) sur l'accord de la religion et de la philosophie, suivi de l'appendice (Dhamī-ma).* 3d ed. Algiers, Editions Carbonel, 1942.
A concise, dependable translation in French by a recognized authority, with the Arabic text, a helpful introduction, and notes. Recommended for use with Hourani's English translation.

Hourani, George F. *On the Harmony of Religion and Philosophy: A Translation, with Introduction and Notes, of Ibn Rushd's Kitāb faṣl al-maqāl, with its Appendix (Damīma) and an Extract from Kitāb al-kashf 'an manāhij al-adilla.* (E. J. W. Gibb Memorial Series.) London, Luzac, 1961.
An accurate translation, faithful to the author's meaning, and especially valuable for its precise, systematic rendering of technical terms. Useful introduction, summaries, and notes.

SECONDARY READINGS

Allard, M. "Le rationalisme d'Averroès d'après une étude sur la création," *Bulletin d'Etudes Orientales,* XIV (1952-54), 7-59.

Arberry, A. J. *Avicenna on Theology.* (Wisdom of the East series.) London, John Murray, 1951.

——— *Revelation and Reason in Islam.* London, Allen and Unwin, 1957; New York, Macmillan, 1957.

Arnaldez, Roger. "La Pensée religieuse d'Averroès," *Studia Islamica,* VII, VIII (1957), X (1959).

Averroes. *Tahāfut al-tahāfut (The Incoherence of the Incoherence),* tr. from the Arabic by Simon van den Bergh. 2 vols. London, Luzac, 1954.

Encyclopaedia of Islam, New Edition. Article "Ibn Rushd" (III, pp. 909-20); and "Falsafa" (III, pp. 769-75).

Gardet, Louis, and M.-M. Anawati, *Introduction à la théologie musulmane.* Paris, J. Vrin, 1948.

Gauthier, L. "Scolastique musulmane et scolastique chrétienne," *Revue d'Histoire de la Philosophie,* II (1928), 221-53; 333-65.

——— *La théorie d'Ibn Rochd (Averroes) sur les rapports de la religion et de la philosophie.* Paris, Leroux, 1909.

Ibn al-Tufail. *The History of Hayy Ibn Yaqzan,* tr. from the Arabic by Simon Ockley and rev. with an introduction by A. S. Fulton. London, Chapman and Hall, 1929; New York, Stokes, 1929.

Maimonides (Moses ben Maimon). *The Guide of the Perplexed,* tr. by Shlomo Pines. University of Chicago Press, 1963. (Also *The Guide for the Perplexed,* tr. from the Arabic by M. Friedländer. 2d ed. London, Routledge, 1904; New York, Dutton, 1904; 4th ed. New York, Dutton, 1927; paperback ed. New York, Dover, 1956.)
The Pines translation has an introduction by Leo Strauss.

Watt, W. M. *Faith and Practice of al-Ghazālī.* London, Allen and Unwin, 1953.

TOPICS FOR DISCUSSION

1. Averroes' concept of philosophy as a "science" and its relation to revelation.

2. The defense of philosophy and the philosophers against the attacks of the theologians.
3. The legal approach of the treatise.
4. Averroes' theory of allegorical interpretation.
5. The view that agreement with philosophy is the ultimate criterion for correct interpretation. Its intellectual and religious implications; the accuracy of philosophy and revelation; the necessity of scripture; the predetermination of the meaning of scripture by philosophical requirements extrinsic to it.
6. The intellectual and moral significance of the doctrine that philosophical interpretations of scripture should not be taught to the majority.
7. Averroes' attitude towards Islam: where does his heart really lie, with Greek philosophy or with Islam?
8. The question of the eternity of God's knowledge.

THE CONFERENCE OF THE BIRDS OF FARĪD AL-DĪN 'AṬṬĀR (*ca.* 1142–*ca.* 1220)

A Persian Sufi who wrote much about man's contemplative journey toward union with God.

TRANSLATIONS

a. COMPLETE

Garcin de Tassy, J. *Mantic Uttair, ou le Langage des Oiseaux.* Paris, L'Imprimerie imperiale, 1863.

b. SELECTIONS

Masani, R. P. *The Conference of the Birds: a Sufi Allegory.* London, Humphrey Milford, 1924.

Nott, C. S. *The Conference of the Birds.* London, Routledge & Kegan Paul, 1961.
A translation from the French of Garcin de Tassy.

Smith, M. *The Persian Mystics: 'Attar.* London, J. Murray, 1932 (Wisdom of the East series)

SECONDARY READINGS

Arberry, A. J. *Muslim Saints and Mystics: Episodes from the Tadhkirat Al-Auliya' ("Memorial of the Saints").* Chicago, University of Chicago Press, 1966.

Ritter, H. *Das Meer der Seele.* Leiden, E. J. Brill, 1955.

TOPICS FOR DISCUSSION

1. 'Aṭṭār's technique: the story as an allegory of the Sufi path.
   a. The role of the Hoopoe.
   b. What the birds represent.
   c. What the valleys represent.
   d. The excuses of the birds.
   e. The function of the anecdotes.
2. 'Aṭṭār's conception of the world; of existence; of the soul.
3. The problem of man's access to God. The role of reason in this quest; the anecdote of the moth and the flame.
4. The significance of the final scene of recognition and union.

THE MYSTICAL POETRY OF JALĀL AL-DĪN RŪMĪ (1207–1273)

The greatest mystical poet of Persia.

TRANSLATIONS

a. COMPLETE: MATHNAVĪ

Nicholson, R. A. *The Mathnawí of Jalálu'ddín Rúmí.* 8 vols. London, Luzac, 1925-40 (E. J. W. Gibb Memorial Series. New Series, 4) Vols. I, III, V text; vols. II, IV, VI translation; vols. VII, VIII commentary.
A literal prose translation, with an extensive commentary and technical notes.

b. SELECTIONS: MATHNAVĪ

Arberry, A. J. *Tales from the Masnavi.* London, Allen and Unwin, 1961.
―――― *More Tales from the Masnavi.* London, Allen and Unwin, 1963.
Nicholson, R. A. *Tales of Mystic Meaning, from the Mathnavi.* London, Chapman and Hall, 1931.
Redhouse, J. W. *The Mesnevī.* London, Trubner, 1881.
A translation of Book I only into rhymed couplets. Very few notes and some inaccuracies.
Whinfield, E. H. *Masnavi i Ma'navi.* 2d ed. London, Trubner, 1898.
A prose translation of selected passages from all six books.
Wilson, C. E. *The Masnavi.* 2 vols. London, Probsthain, 1910.
An accurate prose translation of Book II only with extensive commentary.

c. SELECTIONS: DIVAN OF SHAMS-E TABRIZI

Arberry, A. J. *Mystical Poems of Rūmī.* Chicago, University of Chicago Press, 1968.

Davis, F. H. *The Persian Mystics: Jalalu'd-Din Rumi.* London, J. Murray, 1907. (Wisdom of the East series.)

Nicholson, R. A. *Rumi, Poet and Mystic.* London, Allen and Unwin, 1950 (Ethical and Religious Classics of the East and West.)

———— *Selected Poems from the Dīvāni Shamsi Tabrīz.* Cambridge, Cambridge University Press, 1898; repr. 1952.

d. SELECTIONS: QUATRAINS

Arberry, A. J. *The Rubá'iyāt of Jalāl al-Dīn Rūmī.* London, E. Walker, 1949.

SECONDARY READINGS

Arasteh, R. *Rumi the Persian: Rebirth in Creativity and Love.* Lahore, Ashraf, 1965.

Arberry, A. J. *The Discourses of Rumi.* London, J. Murray, 1961.

Bausani, A. "Theism and Pantheism in Rumi," *Iranian Studies,* I (1967).

Nicholson, R. A. *The Mystics of Islam.* London, Bell, 1914; repr. London, Routledge and Kegan Paul, 1963; Beirut, Khayats, 1966.

Rice, C. *The Persian Sufis.* London, Allen and Unwin, 1964.

Schimmel, A. "The Symbolical Language of Maulānā Jalāl al-Dīn Rūmī," *Studies in Islam,* I (1964).

TOPICS FOR DISCUSSION

1. How does Rūmī present his message? What are his strongest images? Whence are they derived?

2. What does Rūmī mean when he speaks of wine and drunkenness? Of silence?
3. Rūmī's attitude toward reason; the self; this world. How do his attitudes on these matters compare with ʿAṭṭār's on the same subjects?
4. In Rūmī's mysticism, what roles do the following play: love, sacred and profane; the beloved; beauty.
5. What might Rūmī's reaction to al-Ghazālī's *Deliverance from Error* have been?

THE PROLEGOMENA (AL-MUQAD-DIMA) OF IBN KHALDŪN (1332–1406)

One of the most remarkable philosophies of history ever written.

TRANSLATIONS

a. COMPLETE

Rosenthal, Franz. *The Muqaddimah: An Introduction to History.* 3 vols. (Bollingen Series 43.) New York, Pantheon Books, 1958; London, Routledge and Kegan Paul, 1958; Includes a selected bibliography compiled by Walter J. Fischel.

The first complete English translation. Aims at presenting a text comprehensible to the general reader, combining literal translation with a judicious use of modernized terminology.

Slane, W. M. C. de. *Les Prolégomènes historiques d'Ibn Khaldoun,* in *Notices et extraits des manuscrits de la Bibliothèque Nationale* (Académie des Inscriptions et Belles-Lettres), Vols. XIX-XXI. Paris, l'Institut de France, 1862-68. Reissued under the title *Les Prolégomènes d'Ibn Khaldoun* (3 vols.). Paris, Geuthner, 1934-38.

The pioneer translation in French. Highly readable version, freely rendered, but generally faithful to the original.

b. SELECTIONS

Dawood, N. J. *Ibn Khaldūn: the Muqaddimah; an introduction to history.* Princeton, Princeton University Press (Princeton Paperback), 1969.

Excerpts from the Rosenthal translation.

Issawi, Charles. *An Arab Philosophy of History: Selections from the "Prolegomena" of Ibn Khaldun of Tunis.* (The Wisdom of the East series.) London, John Murray, 1950. A selection of brief excerpts rearranged under topical headings and freely rendered in modernized style and terminology, which emphasizes the modern scientific character of the thought of Ibn Khaldūn and presents his ideas on many subjects.

SECONDARY READINGS

Bouthoul, Gaston. *Ibn Khaldoun: sa philosophie sociale.* Paris, Geuthner, 1930.

—— "L'Esprit de corps selon Ibn-Khaldoun," *Revue internationale de sociologie* (Paris), XL (1932), 217-21.

Enan, Muhammad Abdullah. *Ibn Khaldun: His Life and Work,* tr. from the Arabic. Lahore, Ashraf, 1941.

Encyclopaedia of Islam, New Edition. Article "Ibn Khaldūn" (III, pp. 825-31).

Gibb, H. A. R. "The Islamic Background of Ibn Khaldūn's Political Theory," *Bulletin of the School of Oriental Studies* (London) VII (1933-35), 23-31; repr. in Gibb, H. A. R. *Studies on the Civilization of Islam,* ed. by S. J. Shaw and W. R. Polk. Boston, Beacon Press, 1962; paperback ed. 1968; pp. 166-76.

Lacoste, Y. *Ibn Khaldoun; naissance de l'histoire, passé du tiers-monde.* Paris, F. Maspero, 1966. An interesting Marxist interpretation.

Mahdi, Muhsin. *Ibn Khaldūn's Philosophy of History: A Study in the Philosophic Foundation of the Science of Culture.* London, Allen and Unwin, 1957; New York, Macmillan, 1957; paperback ed. Chicago, University of Chicago Press (Phoenix), 1964.

Rosenthal, E. I. J. *Political Thought in Medieval Islam: An Introductory Outline.* Cambridge, Cambridge University Press, 1958; paperback ed. 1962.

See especially pp. 84-109: "The Theory of the Power-State: Ibn Khaldun's Study of Civilization."

Schmidt, Nathaniel. *Ibn Khaldun: Historian, Sociologist, and Philosopher.* New York, Columbia University Press, 1930.

Talbi, M. "Ibn Haldūn et le sens de l'Histoire," *Studia Islamica,* XXVI (1967), 73-148.

TOPICS FOR DISCUSSION

1. The question of Ibn Khaldūn's modernity.
   a. Systematic method and critical approach, as compared to uncritical and uncoordinated accounts of earlier historians.
   b. His contribution of a new technical vocabulary for the description of social phenomena.
   c. His identification of problems which preoccupy modern social sciences today.
   d. His concern with the objective criteria governing social institutions rather than with passing moral judgment on them.
2. His originality, not so much in specific ideas, as in the achievement of a monumental synthesis of Islamic learning with man and his social institutions as its focus.
3. Man in his "ordinary" environment the center of Ibn Khaldūn's thought; Ibn Khaldūn's preoccupation with the end, the good, and the happiness of man; comparison between Ibn Khaldūn's classical concept of the nature of man and society and that of modern science.
4. The supernatural (its divine and magical aspects) in Ibn Khaldūn's thought; the limitation of its influence to the "extraordinary" in human affairs; the relationship between the supernatural and the ordinary forms and functioning of human social institutions.
5. The conflict between reason and revelation as guides to human action; the central problem of Islamic thought. Ibn Khaldūn's reconciliation of the conflict.

6. His concept of *aṣabīya* ("social solidarity" or "group feeling") as the basis of human society; religion as a powerful component of *aṣabīya*.

7. The juxtaposition of nomadic and urban ways of life as a basic polarity of Ibn Khaldūn's thought.

8. The centrality of the state in Ibn Khaldūn's formulation of social, historical, and economic laws; the four phases in the life of a state and the question of their applicability to non-dynastic states.

9. Does Ibn Khaldūn's view of history allow for the cumulative progress of world civilization, or is it purely cyclical in character? What are the possibilities of fundamental reform?

10. "The individual plays a negligible part in Ibn Khaldūn's philosophy; since the individual's tastes and beliefs are conditioned by his environment and education, and since the great men of history have a very minor influence on the course of events" (Issawi, *Ibn Khaldun*, p. 7, note citing Bouthoul).

11. Ibn Khaldūn's disqualification of philosophers as kings.

II. Classics of the Indian Tradition

GENERAL WORKS

BASIC BIBLIOGRAPHIES

Emeneau, M. B. *A Union List of Printed Indic Texts and Translations in American Libraries.* (American Oriental Series, vol. 7.) New Haven, Conn., American Oriental Society, 1935.
A standard reference work listing available translations from Indic languages.

Przyluski, Jean M. Lalou., *et al. Bibliographie bouddhique,* fasc. I-XXXI. Fasç I-III (January, 1928-May, 1931), Paris, Geuthner, 1930-33; fasc. IV-XXXI (May, 1931-May, 1958), Paris, Maissoneuve, 1934-61.
An annotated survey of publications on Buddhism throughout the world from January, 1928, through May, 1958.

Talbot, Phillips, ed. *A Select Bibliography: Asia, Africa, Eastern Europe, Latin America.* New York, American Universities Field Staff, Inc., 1960; Supplement, 1961; pp. 110-48.
A short annotated bibliography of basic books.

INDIAN LITERATURE

Chaitanya, Krishna. *A New History of Sanskrit Literature.* New York, Asia Publishing Co., 1962.
General survey of major works.

De, S. K. *History of Sanskrit Literature.* University of Calcutta, 1947.
Comprehensive survey of the literary works of the classical Indic tradition.

—————— *Sanskrit Poetics as a Study of Aesthetics.* Berkeley, University of California Press, 1963. (The Tagore Memorial Lectures, 1961.)

A good introduction to the major issues of Indian aesthetic theory.

De Bary, Wm. Theodore, ed. *Approaches to the Oriental Classics: Asian Literature and Thought in General Education.* New York, Columbia University Press, 1959.

A collection of essays on various Oriental classics and their significance for general education.

Gargi, Balwant. *Theatre in India.* New York, Theatre Arts Books, 1962.

An introductory survey of Sanskrit drama as well as the popular and modern theater.

Keith, Arthur Berriedale. *A History of Sanskrit Literature.* Oxford, Clarendon Press, 1928.

────── *The Sanskrit Drama: Its Origin, Development, Theory and Practice.* Oxford, Clarendon Press, 1924.

The two titles by Keith are standard works in English on classical Indian literature and dramaturgy.

Macdonell, Arthur A. *A History of Sanskrit Literature.* New York, Appleton, 1900; London, Heinemann, 1900.

Excellent survey of Sanskrit literary works.

Winternitz, Moriz. *A History of Indian Literature,* tr. by Mrs. S. Ketkar and Miss H. Kohn. Vols. I-II, University of Calcutta, 1927-33; vol. I, part 1, 2d. ed., 1959. Vol. III, part 1, Delhi, Motilal Banarsidass, 1963.

The most complete treatment in English of Indian literature.

INDIAN THOUGHT

Brown, William Norman. *Man in the Universe: Some Continuities in Indian Thought.* Berkeley, University of California Press, 1966. (The Tagore Memorial Lectures, 1965.)

A suggestive discussion of major themes in Indian culture.

De Bary, Wm. Theodore, *et al. Sources of Indian Tradition.* New York, Columbia University Press, 1958; paperback ed., 2 vols., 1964.

Edgerton, Franklin. *The Beginnings of Indian Philosophy: A Summing up After a Lifetime of Philological Study and Reflection.* Cambridge, Harvard University Press, 1965.
An introduction to Indian thought, with translations from the Vedas, the Upanishads, the Bhagavad Gita and the Mokshadharma section of the Mahabharata.

Embree, Ainslie, ed. *The Hindu Tradition.* New York, Modern Library, 1966.
An introduction to major aspects of Indian civilization through selected readings.

Farquhar, J. N. *An Outline of the Religious Literature of India.* London, Oxford University Press, 1920.
An excellent survey with good bibliography.

Hastings, James, ed. *Encyclopaedia of Religion and Ethics.* 13 vols. Edinburgh, Clark, 1908-26; New York, Scribner's, 1913-27; 13 vols. in 7, New York, Scribner's, 1951.
The articles on Indic subjects are excellent even though somewhat outdated. The Index (vol. XIII) is quite complete and the location of pertinent Indic themes is easy.

Hopkins, E. Washburn. *Ethics of India.* New Haven, Yale University Press, 1924.
Perhaps the best single volume on Indian ethics.

Potter, Karl H. *Presuppositions of India's Philosophies.* Englewood Cliffs, New Jersey, Prentice-Hall, 1963.
An introduction to the systematic philosophies of India, considered in terms of key topics rather than the traditional "six systems."

Radhakrishnan, Sarvepalli, and Charles A. Moore, eds. *A Source Book in Indian Philosophy.* London, Oxford University Press, 1957; Princeton University Press, 1957.
Useful anthology of Indian philosophical texts. The quality of the translations varies greatly, and Buddhism is weakly represented.

Raghavan, V. *The Indian Heritage: An Anthology of Sanskrit Literature.* Bangalore, Indian Institute of Culture, 1956.

Free translations of Hindu religious works with lengthy introductory survey of basic texts.

Zimmer, Heinrich. *Philosophies of India*, ed. by Joseph Campbell. (Bollingen Series XXVI.) New York, Pantheon Books, 1951; London, Routledge and Kegan Paul, 1951; New York, Noonday Press (Meridian), 1956.
A readable but not always reliable generalization of main themes in Indian thought.

Indian Cultural History and Geography

Basham, Arthur Llewellyn. *The Wonder That Was India: A Survey of the Culture of the Indian Sub-continent Before the Coming of the Muslims*. London, Sidgwick and Jackson, 1954; New York, Grove (Evergreen), 1959.
Excellent coverage of the early period of India's cultural history.

Brown, William Norman, ed. *India, Pakistan, Ceylon*. Ithaca, Cornell University Press, 1950.
Series of articles on India, reprinted from the *Encyclopedia Americana*.

Chavarria-Aguilar, O. L., ed. *Traditional India*. Englewood Cliffs, New Jersey, Prentice-Hall, 1964; paperback ed. also.
Reprints of scholarly articles.

Davies, Cutherbert Collin. *An Historical Atlas of the Indian Peninsula*. Bombay, Oxford University Press, 1949; 2d ed., Madras and Calcutta, Oxford University Press, 1959.
An excellent collection of sketch maps and historical summaries.

Garratt, G. T., ed. *The Legacy of India*. Oxford, Clarendon Press, 1937.
Short essays by various scholars.

Kosambi, D. D. *Ancient India: A History of Its Culture and Civilization*. New York, Pantheon Books, 1966; paperback ed. New York, World (Meridian), 1969.

A provocative social history of ancient India from a Marxist point of view, based on literary, archaeological, and anthropological evidence.

Macdonell, Arthur A. *India's Past: A Survey of Her Literatures, Religions, Languages and Antiquities.* Oxford, Clarendon Press, 1927; Delhi, Banarsidass, 1956.

Brief, authoritative summary of India's cultural history.

Majumdar, R. C., ed. *The History and Culture of the Indian People.* Vols I-VI, IX, X. Bombay, Bharatiya Vidya Bhavan, 1951-1965. Vol. I, *The Vedic Age*, London, Allen and Unwin, 1951.

Covers the period from the Vedic Age to the twentieth century.

Rawlinson, Hugh George. *India: A Short Cultural History.* London, Cresset Press, 1937; New York, Praeger, 1952.

Good general survey.

Renou, Louis, *et al. L'inde classique: Manuel des études indiennes.* 2 vols. Vol. I, Paris, Payot, 1949. Vol. II, Paris, Imprimerie Nationale, 1953. English trans. by Philip Spratt under titles *Classical India* and *Vedic India* (Calcutta, Gupta, 1957).

Comprehensive survey.

THE VEDAS

Ritual hymns that are the earliest source for the fundamental concepts of the Hindu tradition.

TRANSLATIONS

a. COMPLETE

Geldner, Karl F. *Der Rigveda.* (Harvard Oriental Series, Vols. 33-36. Vol. 36: index.) Cambridge, Harvard University Press, 1951-57.
The best complete German translation; includes copious notes, many of which are based on Sayana's Commentary.
Griffith, Ralph T. H. *The Hymns of the Rigveda.* 2 vols. 3d ed. Benares, E. J. Lazarus, 1920-26.
The best complete translation in English. However, the language is archaic and there are numerous errors in the translation itself.

b. SELECTIONS

Bose, Abinash Chandra. *Hymns from the Vedas.* New York, Asia Publishing House, 1966.
A good selection of hymns from the Atharva Veda, the White Yajur Veda and the Sama Veda, as well as the Rig Veda. The verse translations read well but are colored by the editor's personal interpretation of the hymns.
De Bary, Wm. Theodore, *et al. Sources of Indian Tradition.* New York, Columbia University Press, 1958; paperback ed., 2 vols, 1964. Chapter 1.
Only seven of the most representative hymns with introductory comment. Several selections from the *Atharva Veda* are also included in this section.

Edgerton, Franklin. *The Beginnings of Indian Philosophy: A Summing up After a Lifetime of Philological Study and Reflection.* Cambridge, Harvard University Press, 1965.
Rig Veda translations, pp. 51-75; Atharva Veda translations, pp. 79-132.

Macdonell, Arthur A. *Hymns from the Rigveda, Selected and Metrically Translated.* (Heritage of India Series.) London, Oxford University Press, 1922; Calcutta, Association Press, 1922.
Excellent selection and translation.

Max Müller, Friedrich. *Vedic Hymns.* (Sacred Books of the East, vol. 32.) Oxford, Clarendon Press, 1891.
Translations of hymns to the Maruts, Ruda, Vayu, and Vata.

Oldenberg, Hermann. *Vedic Hymns.* (Sacred Books of the East, vol. 46.) Oxford, Clarendon Press, 1897.
Excellent translations of hymns to Agni from books 1-4 of the *Rig Veda.*

Smith, H. Daniel, ed. *Selections from Vedic Hymns.* Berkeley, McCutchan Publishing Corp., 1968. (Paperback)
Selections from the translations of Griffith and from Maurice Bloomfield's translation of the Atharva Veda. (*Hymns of the Atharva Veda,* Sacred Books of the East, Vol. XLII, Oxford, Clarendon Press, 1897.)

Thomas, Edward J. *Vedic Hymns, Translated from the Rigveda.* (Wisdom of the East Series.) London, John Murray, 1923.
Interesting but not very accurate translation of basic hymns.

Zaehner, R. C. *Hindu Scriptures.* New York, Dutton (Everyman's Library), 1966.
Veda selections, pp. 3-12.

SECONDARY READINGS

Bloomfield, Maurice. *The Religion of the Veda: The Ancient Religion of India.* London and New York, Putnam, 1908.

Brown, W. Norman. "The Sources and Nature of *Puruṣa* in the *Puruṣasūkta*," *Journal of the American Oriental Society*, LI (1931), 108-18.

────── "The Ṛigvedic Equivalent for Hell," *Journal of the American Oriental Society*, LXI (1941), 76-80.

────── "The Creation Myth of the Ṛigveda," *Journal of the American Oriental Society*, LXII (1942), 85-98.

────── "Agni, Sun, Sacrifice, and Vāc: A Sacerdotal Ode by Dīrghatamas (Rig Veda 1.164)," *Journal of the American Oriental Society*, LXXXVIII (1968), 199-218.

Four creative scholarly articles on major themes of the Rig Veda.

Keith, Arthur Berriedale. *The Religion and Philosophy of the Veda and Upanishads.* (Harvard Oriental Series, vols. 31, 32.) Cambridge, Harvard University Press, 1925; London, Oxford University Press, 1925.

The standard survey in English.

Macdonell, Arthur A. *Vedic Mythology.* Strassburg, Trübner, 1897. Repr. Varanasi, Indological Book House, 1963.

The best single volume on the Vedic gods.

Renou, Louis. *Religions of Ancient India.* London, Athlone Press, 1953; pp. 1-45. Paperback ed. New York, Schocken, 1968.

TOPICS FOR DISCUSSION

1. The nature of prayer in the *Rig Veda*. The metrical hymns of the *Rig Veda* as literature and scripture.
2. Possible evidence of change and development in the thought within the hymns.
3. Naturalistic polytheism and an elaborate mythology treated henotheistically.
4. Sacrificial rituals, involving Agni and Soma, as links between earthly priests and the gods.
5. Cosmogonic speculations treated in mythological (e.g.,

Indra-Vritra myth), naturalistic (e.g., Heaven-Earth), and abstract (e.g., *puruṣa*, being nonbeing) terms.

6. The place of gods and man in a universe governed by ordinances (*dharma*) and truth (*ṛta*).

UPANISHADS (*ca.* 900–500 B.C.)

The concluding portion of the Vedic texts dealing with, and setting the foundation for, classical Hindu philosophical speculation.

TRANSLATIONS

a. COMPLETE *(Although traditionally there are 108 Upanishads, ten to thirteen are early and fundamental.)*

Deussen, Paul. *Sechzig Upanishads des Veda.* 2d ed. Leipzig, Brockhaus, 1905.
The standard German translation of sixty Upanishads with introductory notes.

Hume, Robert E. *The Thirteen Principal Upanishads.* 2d ed. London, Oxford University Press, 1931.
The best translation into English of the major Upanishads.

Max Müller, Friedrich. *The Upanishads.* (Sacred Books of the East, vols. 1, 15.) Oxford, Clarendon Press, 1879, 1884. (Reprint, New York, Dover Publications, 1961.)
A good but somewhat outdated rendition.

Nikhilananda, Swami. *The Upanishads.* 4 vols. New York, Harper' 1949–59; London, Phoenix House, 1951–59. (Abridged ed., 1 vol., London, Allen and Unwin, 1963; New York, Harper [Torchbook], 1964.;
A translation of the principal Upanishads, with a modern Vedantin interpretation, based on the commentaries of Shankarāchārya.

Radhakrishnan, Sarvepalli. *The Principal Upanishads.* London, Allen and Unwin, 1953; New York, Harper, 1953.
A very useful edition, since the transliterated Sanskrit text is included.

b. SELECTIONS

De Bary, Wm. Theodore, *et al. Sources of Indian Tradition.* New York, Columbia University Press, 1958; paperback ed., 2 vols., 1964. Chapter 3.
A very short but useful translation of several excerpts from the Upanishads with introductory notes.

Edgerton, Franklin. *The Beginnings of Indian Philosophy: A Summing up After a Lifetime of Philological Study and Reflection.* Cambridge, Harvard University Press, 1965; pp. 135-93.

Zaehner, R. C. *Hindu Scriptures.* New York, Dutton (Everyman's Library), 1966; pp. 33-245.
Very readable translations of major portions of the larger Upanishads and complete translations of the smaller Upanishads.

SECONDARY READINGS

Burch, George Bosworth. "The Upanishads," in Wm. Theodore de Bary, ed., *Approaches to the Oriental Classics.* New York, Columbia University Press, 1959; pp. 84-94.
An enthusiastic account by a contemporary philosopher.

Deussen, Paul. *The Philosophy of the Upanishads,* tr. from the German by A. S. Geden. Edinburgh, Clark, 1906. Paperback ed. New York, Dover, 1966.
The principal philosophical concepts of the Upanishads interpreted from the point of view of Shankara's nondualism (*advaita*).

Edgerton, Franklin. "Sources of the Filosofy of the Upanisads," *Journal of the American Oriental Society,* XXXVI (1916), 197-204.
An excellent statement of Upanishadic thought.

―――― *The Bhagavad Gītā.* (Harvard Oriental Series, vol. 39.) Cambridge, Harvard University Press, 1944; London, Oxford University Press, 1944; pp. 3-33.

One of the best summaries of Upanishadic thought as background to the *Bhagavad Gītā.*

Keith, Arthur Berriedale. *Religion and Philosophy of the Veda and Upanishads.* (Harvard Oriental Series, vol. 32.) Cambridge, Harvard University Press, 1925; London, Oxford University Press, 1925. Vol. II, pp. 489-600.

Oldenberg, Hermann. *Die Lehre der Upanishaden und die Anfänge des Buddhismus.* 2d ed. Göttingen, Vandenhoeck and Ruprecht, 1923. An authoritative account of Upanishadic thought as it relates to the development of Buddhism.

Radhakrishnan, Sarvepalli. *The Philosophy of the Upanishads.* 2d ed. London, Allen and Unwin, 1935.

Ranade, R. D. *A Constructive Survey of Upanishadic Philosophy.* Poona, Oriental Book Agency, 1926.

TOPICS FOR DISCUSSION

1. Do the Upanishads represent a systematic philosophical statement or a consistent philosophical viewpoint?

2. Concern for death and the avoidance of transmigration through knowledge and discipline (yoga) with increasing emphasis on monism and monotheism.

3. The equation of two apparently dissimilar elements as a basic characteristic of the Upanishads: e.g., Dawn and the head of the sacrificial horse.

4. The symbolic interpretation of sacrifices and the stress on understanding their meaning rather than on the performance of them; knowledge as power.

5. The methods of dialectical graded teaching and reduction of plurality to unity. Concepts of the nature of the world: the problem of plurality.

6. Investigation of the individual soul or self (*ātman*), its origin, states of consciousness, constituent elements (e.g., breath, intelligence, desire, food, etc.) leading to the identification of universal power (*brahman*) with *ātman.*

MAHĀBHĀRATA (*ca.* 5th cent. B.C.— 4th cent. A.D.)

The longer of the two major Indian epics. This work is primarily a folk epic which includes many religious poems, didactic passages, myths, and legends, and as such is the major encyclopedic source for the significant themes of Indian civilization.

TRANSLATIONS

a. COMPLETE

Dutt, Manmatha Nath, ed. *A Prose English Translation of the Mahabharata.* 8 vols. Calcutta, H. C. Dass, 1895-1905; reprint, New Delhi, 1960.
A fairly good translation of this monumental work.

Ganguli, Kisari Mohan, and Protap Chandra Roy. *The Mahabharata of Krishna-Dwaipayana Vyasa.* 11 vols. Calcutta, Bharata Press, 1883-96; Calcutta, Datta Bose, 1919-30; Calcutta, Oriental Publishing Co., 1956.
An ambitious translation only slightly inferior to that of Dutt. Both are flawed by unidiomatic expressions, but manage to convey something of the grandeur and structure of the original.

b. SELECTIONS

Arnold, Edwin. *Indian Idylls.* Boston, Roberts Brothers, 1883; London, Trübner, 1883.
A blank verse translation of eight stories from the *Mahābhārata,* including the well-known Sāvitrī episode, Nala and Damayantī, the Birth of Death, etc.

Brough, John. *Selections from Classical Sanskrit Literature.*
London, Luzac, 1951; pp. 22-69.
The best prose translation of the popular Sāvitrī episode,
which treats of the ideal faithful Hindu wife and her
conquest of Death.

Dutt, Romesh C. *The Ramayana and the Mahabharata.*
(Everyman's Library.) London, Dent, 1910; New York,
Dutton, 1910.
A rhymed translation of the main episodes of the story.

Lal, P. *The Mahābhārata.* Calcutta, Writers Workshop,
1968–.
A free translation in modern English.

Monier-Williams, M. *Nalopākhyānam: Story of Nala.* 2d ed.
Oxford, Clarendon Press, 1879.
Sanskrit text, accompanied by a metrical English translation
of the famous love story of Nala and Damayantī, by H. H.
Milman.

Narasimhan, C. V. *The Mahābhārata.* New York, Columbia
University Press, 1964.
A literal prose translation of the main story that preserves
the flavor of the original.

Nott, S. C. *The Mahābhārata of Vyasa Krishna Dwaipayana.*
New York, Philosophical Library, 1956; London, James
Press, 1956.
Selected incidents from the Ganguli and Roy translation.

Subramaniam, Kamala. *Mahābhārata.* Bombay, Bharatiya
Vidya Bhavan, 1965.
A prose translation with literary merit.

Yohannan, John D. *A Treasury of Asian Literature.* New
York, John Day, 1956; London, Phoenix House, 1958; New
York, New American Library (Mentor), 1960, pp. 91-111.
A reprint of the Edwin Arnold Translation of the Sāvitrī
story.

SECONDARY READINGS

See below under Secondary Readings for RĀMĀYAṆA *of Vālmīki: Antoine, Hopkins, Macdonell, Monier-Williams, Nivedita, and Vora.*

Fausbøll, M. V. *Indian Mythology, According to the Mahābhārata, in Outline.* London, Luzac, 1903.

'Ghoshal, U. N. *A History of Indian Political Ideas: The Ancient Period and the Period of Transition to the Middle Ages.* London, Oxford University Press, 1959.

Hopkins, E. Washburn. *The Great Epic of India.* New York, Scribner's, 1901.

———— *Legends of India.* New Haven, Yale University Press, 1928.

A poetical "reinterpretation" of several popular legends.

Jacobi, Hermann. *Mahābhārata Inhaltsangabe, Index und Concordanz der Calcuttaer und Bombayer Ausgaben.* Bonn, Friedrich Cohen, 1903.

A survey of the contents, plus a comprehensive indext to the epic.

Macdonell, Arthur A. *A History of Sanskrit Literature.* New York, Appleton, 1900; pp. 277-98.

A short but scholarly statement of the origin of the epic, its date, and the main narrative and episodes.

Sharma, Ram Karan. *Elements of Poetry in the Mahābhārata.* Berkeley, University of California Press, 1964.

Sukthanker, V. S. *On the Meaning of the Mahābhārata.* Bombay, Asiatic Society of Bombay, 1957.

Four papers on aspects of the epic by the general editor of the critical edition of the *Mahābhārata.*

TOPICS FOR DISCUSSION

1. The *Mahābhārata* as an epic in its Indian context: localization of place, but not of time; the secret of its great

national appeal through easily identifiable motifs and symbols; allegorical qualities, especially in the Krishna legends.

2. A living mythology: men and gods as part of an ordered scheme of life; the character of its chief figures: men or gods?

3. Concept of the hero.

4. The expression of human emotions; married love and devotion.

5. The ethics of the *Mahābhārata*; chivalry and the warrior's code; group loyalty.

6. Attitudes towards fate and death.

7. The importance of asceticism and the power of vows, curses, and truth (*satya*).

8. The function of kingship and the social order.

BHAGAVADGĪTĀ (*ca.* 100 B.C.-A.D. 100)

The BHAGAVADGĪTĀ *is a religious and philosophic synthesis of many aspects of Indian thought. It is the central text of Hindu devoion as well as the classic statement of Hindu social ethics.*

TRANSLATIONS

Arnold, Edwin. "The Song Celestial" (text of 2d ed., 1886), in Franklin Edgerton, *The Bhagavad Gītā.* (Harvard Oriental Series, vol. 39.) Cambridge, Harvard University Press, 1944; London, Oxford University Press, 1944.
A literary translation in blank verse at the expense of literal accuracy. This version is available in numerous other editions, including the following: Allahabad, Kitabistan, 1944; Bombay, Jaico, 1957.

Barnett, Lionel D. *Bhagavad-gītā, or, The Lord's Song.* London, Dent, 1905 (reprinted, 1920). Also in Nicol Macnicol, ed., *Hindu Scriptures: Hymns from the Rigveda, Five Upanishads, the Bhagavadgita.* (Everyman's Library.) London, Dent, 1957; New York, Dutton, 1957; pp. 225-87. (Originally published 1938.)
A scholarly translation.

Chatterji, Mohini M. *The Bhagavad Gītā, or, The Lord's Lay.* London, Trübner, 1887; Boston, Ticknor, 1887; reprinted, with an essay by Ainslie T. Embree, New York, Julian Press, 1960.
A devotional translation with numerous textual comparisons with the Bible.

Deussen, Paul. *Vier philosophische Texte de Mahābhāratam.* Leipzig, Brockhaus, 1906.

An excellent German translation of the *Bhagavadgītā, Moksadharma, Anugītā,* and *Sanatsujātīya.* The *Bhagavadgītā* was published separately as *Der Gesang des Heiligen: eine philosophische Episode des Mahābhāratam* (Leipzig, Brockhaus, 1911).

Deutsch, Eliot. *The Bhagavad Gītā.* New York, Harcourt, Brace, 1968; paperback ed. also.

Readable translation intended for academic use.

Edgerton, Franklin. *The Bhagavad Gītā.* (Harvard Oriental Series, vol. 38.) Cambridge, Harvard University Press, 1944; London, Oxford University Press, 1944; New York, Harper (Torchbook), 1964.

The most accurate English translation.

Garbe, Richard. *Die Bhagavadgītā.* 2d ed. Leipzig, H. Haessel, 1921.

An excellent German translation with a fine introductory essay discussing the original form of the text, the development of the Bhagavata religion, and the teachings of the *Gītā.*

Hill, W. Douglas P. *The Bhagavadgītā.* London, Oxford University Press, 1928. 2d, abridged ed. (lacking Sanskrit text). Madras, Oxford University Press, 1953.

Accurate translation, with particular emphasis on the religious context of the work. Extensive critical notes and an excellent introduction.

Mascaro, Juan. *The Bhagavad Gītā.* Baltimore, Penguin Books, 1962.

A prose translation of little value.

Nikhilananda, Swami. *The Bhagavad Gita.* New York, Ramakrishna-Vivekananda Center, 1944.

A devotional translation with copious notes by the translator and references on each stanza to Shankara's commentary.

Otto, Rudolf. *The Original Gītā: The Song of the Supreme*

Exalted One, tr. from the German by J. E. Turner. London, Allen and Unwin, 1939.

A theological study of the work with emphasis on the devotional elements, based on principles of textual analysis suggested by Richard Garbe.

Paramananda, Swami. *Srimad-Bhagavad-gita, or, The Blessed Lord's Song.* Boston, Vedanta Centre, 1913. Reprinted in Lin Yutang, *The Wisdom of China and India.* New York, Random House, 1942; pp. 54-114.

A translation of dubious worth.

Prabhavananda, Swami, and Christopher Isherwood. *Bhagavadgita, the Song of God.* Hollywood, Marcel Rodd, 1944; London, Phoenix House, 1947; New York, Harper, 1951. Also published under title: *The Song of God: Bhagavad-Gita.* New York, New American Library (Mentor), 1959.

This translation aims at giving a message to the modern reader, rather than presenting the original meaning of the *Gītā.*

Radhakrishnan, Sarvepalli. *The Bhagavadgītā.* London, Allen and Unwin, 1948; New York, Harper, 1948; 2d ed., London, Allen and Unwin, 1956.

Influenced by other existing versions, but valuable for its verse by verse commentary giving references to world philosophical and religious thought.

Ryder, Arthur W. *The Bhagavad-Gita.* University of Chicago Press, 1929.

A rhyming, but rather faithful, translation.

Telang, Kashināth Trimbak. *The Bhagavadgītā, with the Sanatsujātīya and the Anugītā.* (Sacred Books of the East, vol. 8) Oxford, Clarendon Press, 1882.

The best translation by a believing Hindu. It includes two similar philosophical or religious texts of the *Mahābhārata.*

Zaehner, R. H. *Hindu Scriptures.* New York, Dutton (Everyman's Library), 1966; pp. 249-325.

Coherent, readable English translation.

SECONDARY READINGS

Most of the translations cited above contain useful introductory or commentarial material.

Aurobindo, Ghose (Sri Aurobindo). *Essays on the Gītā.* New York, Dutton, 1950.

A detailed analysis of the concepts of the *Bhagavadgītā*, from the philosophical rather than historical or philological point of view, by one of modern India's most provocative thinkers.

Bhave, Vinoba. *Talks on the Gita.* New York, Macmillan, 1960; London, Allen and Unwin, 1960.

A series of eighteen short essays on the message of the *Bhagavadgītā* for modern life. These essays were originally talks given to Bhave's fellow prisoners in 1932 during the Indian independence movement.

Buitenen, J. A. B. van. *Rāmānuja on the Bhagavadgītā: A Condensed Rendering of his Gītā bhāṣya.* The Hague, H. L. Smits, 1953.

An excellent scholarly translation of one of the most important classical Hindu commentators on the *Bhagavadgītā.*

Dasgupta, Surendra Nath. *A History of Indian Philosophy.* Cambridge University Press, 1932. Vol. II, pp. 437-552.

A provocative study of basic philosophical ideas of the *Bhagavadgītā.*

Desai, Mahadev. *The Gospel of Selfess Action, or, The Gita According to Gandhi.* Ahmedabad, Navjivan Publishing House, 1956.

Introductory essays by both author and translator give insights into Gandhi's own unorthodox interpretations of Hinduism as well as indicate the meaning the *Gītā* has for the more orthodox.

Edgerton, Franklin. *The Bhagavad Gītā.* (Harvard Oriental Series, vol. 39). Cambridge, Harvard University Press, 1944; London, Oxford University Press, 1944.

Short critical essays on the background, philosophy, religion, and significant concepts of the text, based on internal and historical evidence.

Gandhi, Mohandas Karamchand. See above, under Desai, Mahadev.

Jñānadeva (Jñāneśvara, also known as Shri Dnyānadev). *Bhāvārtha-Dīpikā, Otherwise Known as Dnyāneshwarī*, tr. by R. K. Bhagwat, rev. by S. V. Pandit and V. V. Dixit. 2 vols. Poona, Dnyaneshwari English Rendering Publishing Association, 1953-54.

—— *Gita Explained, by Dnyaneshwar Maharaj*, tr. into English by Manu Subedar. 3d ed. Bombay, Manu Subedar, 1945.

Two versions of the important commentary on the *Bhagavadgītā* by a medieval Hindu saint. The translation by R. K. Bhagwat is complete and superior.

Kalyāna-Kalpataru, "*Gītā* Number," Vol. II (no. 1, January, 1935.)

A collection of short essays of varying value on various concepts of the *Bhagavadgītā*, mostly by believing Hindus.

Roy, Satis Chandra. *The Bhagavad-Gītā and Modern Scholarship*. London, Luzac, 1941.

An illuminating historical study of critical interpretations and background aspects of the *Bhagavadgītā*.

Tilak, B. G. *Śrimad Bhagavadītā Rahasya*. 2 vols. Poona, R. B. Tilak, 1935-36.

TOPICS FOR DISCUSSION

1. Arjuna's question: the social results of personal actions as a reflection of basic problems of human existence.
2. Krishna's answer in terms of the relation of action to the real self.
3. Concepts of individual duty or social obligation (*dharma*), social class (*varna*), individual action (*karma*), and the problem of free will.

4. Nature (*prakṛti*) and Spirit (*puruṣa*): concept of nature or matter with its qualities (*guṇa*); the relation of man to the world.

5. Ways to release: concept of yoga; discipline of action, sacrifice, knowledge, meditation, and devotion.

6. Philosophical synthesis: Sāṁkhya cosmology, yoga practice, Vedānta metaphysics.

7. Nature of the Godhead: Krishna as an incarnation (*avatāra*) of Vishnu; concept of Brahman; supreme spirit (*puruṣa*); preeminent manifestations and universal form of the Godhead.

8. The appeal of the *Gītā* in both the East and the West.

RĀMĀYANA OF VĀLMĪKI (ca. 200 B.C.)

The earlier of the two major Indian epics and the best known of all Indian legends. This work is primarily an artificial or court epic which forms the basis for many later religious texts.

TRANSLATIONS

a. COMPLETE

Griffith, Ralph T. H. *The Rámáyan of Valmiki.* 5 vols. London, Trübner, 1870–74; Benares, E. J. Lazarus and Co., 1870-74; reprinted, London, Luzac, 1895; Benares, Lazarus, 1895.
A good verse translation which, in spite of somewhat archaic language, preserves much of the flavor of the original.

Sen, Makhan Lal. *The Ramayan: A Modernized Version in English Prose.* 3 vols. Calcutta, Bose, 1927. 3d ed., Calcutta, Mukhopadhyay (Firma K. L. M), n.d.
A free and often inaccurate translation of dubious worth.

Shastri, Hari Prasad. *The Ramayana of Valmiki.* 3 vols. London, Shanti Sadan, 1952-59.
The best available prose translation. The rendition is fairly reliable as well as readable. Detailed glossaries of Sanskrit proper names and epithets are included in each volume.

b. SELECTIONS

Dutt, Romesh C. *The Ramayana and the Mahabharata.* (Everyman's Library.) London, Dent, 1910; New York, Dutton, 1910; reprinted 1929.

A fairly good, but somewhat monotonous, metrical translation of the main narrative elements of the epic. In many respects, this is a useful abridgment.

Lin Yutang, ed. *The Wisdom of China and India.* New York, Random House, 1942; New York, Modern Library (paperback), 1955; pp. 135-262. (Also published in two volumes, *The Wisdom of China* and *The Wisdom of India,* London, Michael Joseph, 1944.)

An abridgment of the Dutt translation.

Raghavan, V. *The Indian Heritage.* Bangalore, Indian Institute of Culture, 1956; pp. 150-292.

A free prose translation of the main narrative elements.

SECONDARY READINGS

Antoine, Robert. "Indian and Greek Epics," in Wm. Theodore de Bary, ed., *Approaches to the Oriental Classics.* New York, Columbia University Press, 1959; pp. 95-112. "Comments on the *Rāmāyana* and *Mahābhārata*" by George T. Artola, pp. 113-18.

Hopkins, Edward Washburn. *Epic Mythology.* Strassburg, Trübner, 1915.

A standard, scholarly reference work on the Indian epics, with detailed index of deities, sages, etc.

Jacobi, Hermann. *The Rāmāyana,* tr. from the German by S. N. Ghosal. Baroda, Oriental Institute, 1960.

Analytical study of the epic, with special concern for the origin and composition of the text.

Macdonell, Arthur A. *A History of Sanskrit Literature.* New York, Appleton, 1900; pp. 302-17 *passim.*

Menen, Aubrey. *The Ramayana.* New York, Scribner's, 1954; paperback reprint, n.d. Also under title *Rama Retold;* London, Chatto and Windus, 1954.

A satirical recreation of the Indian epic featuring originality of interpretation rather than fidelity to tradition.

Monier-Williams, M. *Indian Epic Poetry*. London, Williams and Norgate, 1863.
An excellent account of the epics with comparative references to Western literature.

Narayan, R. K. *The Rāmāyana: A Shortened Modern Prose Version of the Indian Epic Suggested by the Tamil Version of Kamban*. New York, Viking, 1972.
An Indian novelist's recreation of the Tamil epic which was based on Vālmīki's.

Nivedita, Sister (Margaret E. Noble), and Ananda K. Coomaraswamy. *Myths of the Hindus and Buddhists*. London, Harrap, 1913; New York, Holt, 1914; New York, Farrar and Rinehart, 1934; pp. 6-117.
A short prose retelling of the major episodes of the *Rāmāyana*.

Srivivasa Sastri, V. S. *Lectures on the Rāmāyana*. Madras, Madras Sanskrit Academy, 1949; rev. ed. 1961.

Vora, Dhairyabala P. *Evolution of Morals in the Epics*. Bombay, Popular Book Depot, 1959.
A very good survey of marriage customs, *karma*, and socioethical concepts in the *Rāmāyana* and *Mahābhārata*.

TOPICS FOR DISCUSSION

1. The *Rāmāyana* as a court epic: scope of the work in terms of geography and time; alternation between urban and forest environments; intrigues, tournaments, and wars.
2. The *Rāmāyana* as a dramatic tragedy, history, and allegory.
3. Levels of interpretation: the role of fate or destiny; personal responsibility for action. Mythological and supernatural elements and their relationship to human life.
4. The plot and narrative as contributing factors to dramatic tension.
5. Typical Hindu motifs: a Brahman's curse; asceticism and

hermitages; the socially ordered life; concept of truth (*satya*) as the ultimate criterion for action; didactic elements.

6. Descriptions of battles and nature as contributing to the literary merit of the work.

7. Characters of Rāma and Sītā: real people or idealized concepts?; the role of human feelings and emotions; Rāma as king or god; Sītā as an ideal wife; Sītā's ordeals.

8. The roles and characters of secondary characters such as Rāvana, Lakshmana, Hanumān.

9. Factors contributing to the popular appeal of the *Rāmāyana*.

YOGA SŪTRAS OF PATAÑJALI (*ca.* A.D. 300)

The classical Hindu philosophical treatise on the discipline of yoga, which, though one of the oldest concepts of Indian civilization, is today attracting the serious attention of the Western world.

TRANSLATIONS

Hauer, J. W. *Der Yoga als Heilweg.* Stuttgart, Kohlhammer, 1932.

———— *Der Yoga, ein indischer Weg zum Selbst.* Stuttgart, Kohlhammer, 1958. A 2d, completely revised edition of *Der Yoga als Heilweg.*

A careful, quite accurate, German translation of the *Yoga Sūtras* is included in these volumes.

Prabhavananda, Swami, and Christopher Isherwood. *How to Know God: The "Yoga Aphorisms" of Patanjali.* New York, Harper, 1953; London, Allen and Unwin, 1953.

A very readable, but not always accurate, translation, with the authors' comments on each sūtra and a lengthy introduction.

Prasada, Rama. *Patanjali's Yoga Sutras.* (Sacred Books of the Hindus, vol. 4.) 3d ed. Allahabad, Panini Office, 1924. (1st ed., 1910.)

A defective translation with obscure renderings of the *Yoga Sutras.* This volume, however, is enhanced by the inclusion of Vyasa's commentary (*bhāsya*) and Vācaspati's gloss, both of which are better translations.

This translation, slightly revised, is reproduced in Sarvepalli Radhakrishnan and Charles A. Moore, eds., *A Source Book in Indian Philosophy* (London, Oxford University Press, 1957; Princeton University Press, 1957), pp. 435-85, with excerpts from the commentaries.

Raghavan, V. *The Indian Heritage.* Bangalore, Indian Institute of Culture, 1956; pp. 141-49.

A very free, running translation—virtually a paraphrase—of the sutras. The translation, while readable, is incomplete.

Vivekananda, Swami. *Rāja Yoga, or, Conquering the Internal Nature.* Calcutta, Swami Trigunatita, 1901; London, Luzac, 1937; 2d ed. rev., New York, Ramakrishna-Vivekananda Center, 1956. Also in Lin Yutang, *The Wisdom of China and India* (New York, Random House, 1942), pp. 115-32, and Swami Nikhilananda, ed., *Vivekananda: The Yogas and Other Works,* rev. ed. (New York, Ramakrishna-Vivekananda Center, 1953), pp. 577-694.

This translation (first published in 1899) is quite readable and fairly accurate. Each sūtra is commented upon by the Swami in the light of his neo-Vedantic orientation.

Weiler, Royal W. *Patañjali's Yogasūtras.* (Dittographed; Committee on Oriental Studies, Columbia University.)

Exact, scholarly translation with a good introduction.

Woods, James Haughton. *The Yoga-System of Patañjali, or the Ancient Hindu Doctrine of Concentration of Mind, Embracing the Mneomonic Rules, Called Yoga-Sūtras, of Patañjali.* (Harvard Oriental Series, vol. 17.) 2d ed. Cambridge, Harvard University Press, 1927.

This edition includes a fairly accurate translation of Veda-Vyāsa's commentary and Vācaspati's *Tattva-vaiśāradī* (gloss).

The translation of the sutras themselves is accurate, but not readily comprehensible.

———— "The Yoga-Sūtras of Patañjali as Illustrated by the Comment Entitled The Jewel's Lustre or Maniprabhā," *Journal of the American Oriental Society,* XXXIV (1914), 1-114.

In several respects this edition, with its commentary, is superior to the preceding. It is somewhat more readable.

SECONDARY READINGS

Behanan, Kovoor T. *Yoga: A Scientific Evaluation.* New York, Macmillan, 1937; London, Secker and Warburg, 1937; New York, Dover, 1960.
A provocative analysis of yoga practice in the light of modern Western scientific standards, especially those of psychology and psychoanalysis.
Coster, Geraldine. *Yoga and Western Psychology: A Comparison.* London, Oxford University Press, 1934, reprinted 1945.
A comparative study of the *Yoga Sūtras* of Patañjali in terms of Western psychology, especially the theories of Freud and Jung.
Dasgupta, Surendranath. *Yoga as Philosophy and Religion.* London, Kegan Paul, Trench, Trubner, 1924; New York, Dutton, 1924.
A commentary on Patañjali's *Yoga Sūtras* on the basis of traditional commentaries. The emphasis is on metaphysics, ethics, and practice.
———— *History of Indian Philosophy.* 4 vols. Cambridge, University Press, 1932-49. Vol. I, pp. 208-73.
A scholarly analysis of the fundamental principles of the Sāṁkhya and yoga philosophies.
Eliade, Mircea. *Yoga: Immortality and Freedom,* tr. from the French by Willard R. Trask. New York, Pantheon Books, 1958; London, Routledge and Kegan Paul, 1958.
A comprehensive survey of yoga, its origin and development. There are several minor philological inaccuracies in this detailed work.
Gervis, Pearce. *Naked They Pray.* London, Cassell, 1956; New York, Duell, Sloan and Pearce, 1957.

An unpretentious personal account of the author's contact with yogis in northwest India. These experiences are described with admirable simplicity and open-mindedness.

Hopkins, E. Washburn. "Yoga-Technique in the Great Epic," *Journal of the American Oriental Society*, XXII (1901), 333-79.
An excellent account of the concept of yoga as it appears in the *Mahābhārata* prior to its formulation into a philosophical system by Patañjali.

Sivananda, Swami. *Practice of Bhakti-Yoga*. Amritsar, 1937.
This is perhaps the best of the countless books on the practical application of the ancient Indian concept of yoga to the life of modern Western man.

——— *Practical Lessons in Yoga*. Lahore, Motilal Banarsi Dass, 1938.

Wood, Ernest. *Yoga*. Baltimore and Harmondsworth, Penguin Books, 1959.
A fairly good survey of the yoga concept with reference to numerous texts, especially Patañjali's *Yoga Sūtra*. The interpretation is not always in accord with textual evidence, but the work has many useful qualities.

Woodroffe, Sir John G. (Arthur Avalon, pseud.). *The Serpent Power*. London, Luzac, 1919; 2d ed. rev., Madras, Ganesh, 1924; 5th ed. enl., Madras, Ganesh, 1953.
A translation and commentary on two short post-Patañjali yoga texts dealing with *laya-yoga*, which is concerned primarily with psychic energy and psychic centers in the body. There is a lengthy introduction discussing the theoretical details of the practice.

TOPICS FOR DISCUSSION

1. Psychological aspects: the nature of the mind (*citta*) or thought, its activities (*vṛtti*) or fluctuations; the senses; residual impressions (the subconscious).

2. The control of the mind through yoga discipline: the eight-limbs; the importance of dispassion or asceticism and regular practice.
3. Meditation: the practice of controlled contemplation (*saṁyama*), including stages of concentration (*dhāraṇā*), meditation (*dhyāna*), and trance (*samādhi*). Physical and psychological obstacles to meditation.
4. The nature of trance (*samādhi*).
5. Philosophical elements: the spirit (*puruṣa*) or "Seer" entangled in matter or nature (*prakṛti*) based on dualistic Sāṁkhya (cf. *Bhagavadgītā*, above); the concept of God (*iśvara*).
6. The goal of yoga as "isolation."
7. The significance of supernatural powers in the course of yoga practice.
8. The place of ethics and morality in the *Yoga Sūtras*.

THE VEDĀNTA SŪTRA WITH THE COMMENTARY OF SHANKĀR-ĀCHĀRYA (*ca.* 780–820)

Shankarāchārya, or Shankara, is the most influential of Indian philosophers. His nondualistic (advaita) philosophy, based on the latter portion of the Vedas, i.e., the UPANISHADS *(Vedānta), is the form of Indian thought best known in the West.*

TRANSLATIONS

Apte, Vasudeo Mahadeo. *Brahma-sūtra Shankara-bhāshya.* Bombay, Popular Book Depot, 1960.
An accurate and readable translation of Shankara's commentary on the *Brahma Sūtras.*

Deussen, Paul. *Die Sūtra's des Vedānta, oder die Çārīraka-Mīmānsā des Bādarāyana, nebst dem vollständigen Commentare des Çañkāra.* Leipzig, Brockhaus, 1887.
An excellent German translation of Shankara's commentary by a leading Western authority on the Vedānta philosophy.

Thibaut, George. *The Vedānta-Sūtras of Bādarāyana, with the Commentary by Śankara.* (Sacred Books of the East, vols. 34, 38) Oxford, Clarendon Press, 1890. 2 vols. New York, Dover Publications, 1962.
This is still probably the best complete translation in English.

SECONDARY READINGS

Dasgupta, Surendranath. *History of Indian Philosophy.* Cam-

bridge University Press, 1932. Vol. I, pp. 406-94; Vol. II, pp. 1-82.
A detailed survey of the main philosophical problems of the Vedānta system according to Shankara.
—— *Indian Idealism.* Cambridge University Press, 1933; pp. 149-98.
A short, somewhat generalized discussion of the Vedānta and related systems as idealism.
Deussen, Paul. *The System of the Vedānta,* tr. from the German by Charles Johnston. Chicago, Open Court, 1912.
A systematic and detailed study of the Vedānta as expressed in the *Brahma Sūtras* and Shankara's commentary. This is probably the best book available on the subject.
—— *Outline of the Vedanta System of Philosophy, According to Shankara,* tr. from the German by J. H. Woods and C. B. Runkle. London, Oxford University Press, 1927; Cambridge, Harvard University Press, 1927.
A short but very useful essay on the concepts of Vedānta in terms of theology, cosmology, psychology, migration of the soul, and emancipation.
Deutsch, Eliot. *Advaita Vedānta: A Philosophical Reconstruction.* Honolulu, East-West Center Press, 1969.
The insights of modern western philosophy are used to elucidate the meaning of the Indian system.
Ghate, V. S. *The Vedānta.* Poona, Bhandarkar Oriental Research Institute, 1926; 2d ed., 1960.
An excellent critical analysis of the classical commentaries of Shankara, Rāmanūja, Nimbārka, Madhva, and Vallabha on the *Brahma Sūtras.* This scholarly study differentiates the five classical schools of Vedānta based on their respective interpretations.
Mahadevan, T. M. P. *Gaudapāda: A Study in Early Advaita.* Madras, University of Madras Press, 1952.
A scholarly study of the major pre-Shankara Vedantin that illuminates Shankara's dialectics.

Max Müller, Friedrich. *The Vedanta Philosophy.* Calcutta, Susil Gupta, 1955. Originally published as *Three Lectures on the Vedanta Philosophy* (London, Longmans, 1894.)
A series of three essays (originally lectures) on the origin of Vedānta, its treatment of the soul and god, and similarlities and differences between Indian and European philosophy.

Menon, Y. Keshava and R. F. Allen, *The Pure Principle; an Introduction to the Philosophy of Shankara.* East Lansing, Michigan State University Press, 1960.

Radhakrishnan, Sarvepalli. *The Brahma Sūtra, the Philosophy of Spiritual Life.* New York, Harper, 1960; London, Allen and Unwin, 1960.
A translation of the *Brahma Sūtras* with references to the various commentaries as well as translator's remarks. There is a lengthy introduction.

Shankarāchāraya. *Upadésāsahasrī: A Thousand Teachings,* tr. by Swami Jagadananda. 1st ed., Hollywood, Vedanta Society of Southern California, 1949; 3d ed. Mylapore and Madras, Sri Ramakrishna Math, 1961.
A considerably shorter work than the commentary on the *Brahma Sūtras,* this text sets forth Shankara's philosophy somewhat more concisely. The work is written in both prose and verse.

Thibaut, George. *The Vedānta-Sūtras, with the Commentary of Rāmānuga.* (Sacred Books of the East, vol. 48.) Oxford, Clarendon Press, 1904.
An excellent translation of Rāmānuja's commentary, which is second only to Shankara's in importance to the Vedānta.

Vivekananda, Swami. *Jñāna Yoga.* 2d ed. rev. New York, Ramakrishna-Vivekananda Center, 1955. Also in Swami Nikhilananda, ed. *Vivekananda: The Yogas and Other Works.* New York, Ramakrishna-Vivekananda Center, 1953; pp. 201-399.
The essays on *māya* and "practical Vedānta" are particularly illuminating.

TOPICS FOR DISCUSSION

1. Shankara's interpretation of the Upanishads in terms of nonduality (advaita) or a monistic system of philosophy.

2. The use of scriptural authority and exegesis to eliminate ignorance, refute contrary philosophies (*e.g.*, Buddhism, Sāṃkhya, etc.), and reconcile textual inconsistencies.

3. The nature of the Self (*ātman*) and its involvement with the senses; "superimposition"; the function of intelligence (*buddhi*) or reason as a means to release (*mokṣa*); the Self in dream and deep sleep.

4. The nature of ignorance (*avidyā*) or nescience; its origin in the concept of illusion (*māya*) and its removal through the knowledge of Brahman. The impossibility that those who know reality can be aware of ignorance.

5. The individual soul (*jīva*) and god (*īśvara*) in terms of bondage (*saṃsāra*) and release (*mokṣa*); the meaning of "That thou art" (*tat tvam asi*); the place of devotion in this context.

6. The problem of cause and effect: how can they be identical?

7. The ethical implication of Shankara's philosophy: moral prerequisites to undertaking the study of Vedanta; the relation of action to knowledge; the concept of a single, unitary Self as a basis for moral action; the social behavior of a liberated man.

THERAVĀDA BUDDHISM:
THE TIPIṬAKA

*The canon of Buddhist texts in Pali is the oldest complete and
extant collection of Buddhist scriptures. It belongs to one of
the earliest traditions within Buddhism, the "Way of the
Elders"* (Theravāda). *This tradition is still dominant in
Ceylon, Burma, Thailand, and Cambodia. The canon itself—
the "Three Baskets"* (TIPIṬAKA)—*is a lengthy anthology of
the Buddha's teachings in three parts: the* VINAYA-PIṬAKA,
*which consists of the rules of discipline for monks and nuns
and narrations of the incidents which prompted the Buddha to
declare those rules; the* SUTTA-PIṬAKA, *containing the doctrin-
al utterances of the Buddha; and, the* ABHIDHAMMA-PIṬAKA,
a repository of scholastic analyses of the doctrines. The
SUTTA-PIṬAKA, *the heart of the canon, is subdivided into five
collections. The criteria of division are the length of the
discourses and their method of arrangement: the Long
Discourses; the Middle-length Discourses; the Connected
Discourses; the Discourses Arranged by Numerical Progression; and, the Minor Discourses.*

TRANSLATIONS

*The entire Pāli Canon, along with much of the standard
commentary, has been edited and translated into English by
scholars affiliated with London's Pali Text Society. Also,
there are many anthologies of canonical and paracanonical
Theravada literature, among which the following are the most
useful:*

Burlingame, Eugene Watson. *Buddhist Parables.* New Haven,
    Yale University Press, 1922.

A well-balanced anthology with excellent original translations. A few texts from the Sanskrit and some European parallels are included.

Burtt, Edwin Arthur. *The Teachings of the Compassionate Buddha.* New York, New American Library (Mentor), 1955.
A useful anthology of texts drawn from the works of various translators. Mahāyāna sources are also included. Emphasis is on the conceptual and devotional aspects of Buddhism.

Conze, Edward. *Buddhist Meditation.* London, Allen and Unwin, 1956; New York, Macmillan, 1956.
A good anthology dealing with devotion, mental training, and the concept of wisdom as represented in Buddhism.

—— *Buddhist Scriptures.* Harmondsworth and Baltimore, Penguin Books, 1959.
The translations are original and modern. Mahāyāna texts are also included.

——, *et al. Buddhist Texts Through the Ages.* New York, Philosophical Library, 1954; Oxford, B. Cassirer, 1954.
Texts illustrating the basic concepts of Buddhism with emphasis on the Mahāyāna teachings.

De Bary, Wm. Theodore, *et al. Sources of Indian Tradition.* New York, Columbia University Press, 1958; pp. 93-202. (Paperback ed., 2 vols., 1964.)
The translations of Buddhist texts by A. L. Basham are short but representative of the principles of the Theravāda, Mahāyāna, and Vajrayāna forms of Buddhism.

Hamilton, Clarence H. *Buddhism, a Religion of Infinite Compassion: Selections from Buddhist Literature.* New York, Liberal Arts, 1952.
A selection from Pāli, Sanskrit, Chinese, Japanese, and Tibetan texts.

Rhys-Davids, Thomas William. *Buddhist Suttas.* (Sacred Books of the East, vol. 11.) Oxford, Clarendon Press, 1881.
A very good translation of seven basic *suttas* (discourses) of Theravāda Buddhism. The important First Sermon (*Dhammacakkappavattana Sutta*) is included.

Thomas, Edward J. *The Road to Nirvana: A Selection of the Buddhist Scriptures.* London, John Murray, 1950.
A short anthology of Theravāda texts. The translations are quite competent. Some *Jātakas* (birth stories) are included.
Warren, Henry Clarke. *Buddhism in Translation.* (Harvard Oriental Series, vol. 3.) Cambridge, Harvard University Press, 1896; student's ed., 1953. (Republished, New York, Atheneum, 1963.)
Probably the best anthology of Pāli texts. Unfortunately the First Sermon is not included and there is some repetition of the basic concepts presented.

SECONDARY READINGS

Bapat, Purushottam Vishvanath. *2500 Years of Buddhism.* Delhi, Publications Division, Ministry of Information and Broadcasting, Government of India, 1956.
Comprehensive collection of articles, mostly by Indian scholars. Glossary, bibliography, maps, and illustrations are included.
Conze, Edward. *Buddhism: Its Essence and Development.* New York, Philosophical Library, 1951; Oxford, B. Cassirer, 1951; New York, Harper (Torchbook), 1959.
Good survey of the major schools of Buddhism.
Coomaraswamy, Ananda K. *Buddha and the Gospel of Buddhism.* New York, Putnam 1916; London, Harrap, 1916; Bombay, Asia Publishing House, 1956.
Discussion of the teachings of Buddhism. Buddhist art, sculpture, painting, and literature are also treated.
Edgerton, Franklin. "Did the Buddha Have a System of

Metaphysics?", *Journal of the American Oriental Society,* LXXIX (1959), 81-85.
Criticism of Hermann Oldenberg's *Buddha,* which is listed below.

Foucher, A. *The Life of the Buddha According to the Ancient Texts and Monuments of India.* Abridged translation by Simone Brangier Boas. Middletown, Conn., Wesleyan University Press, 1963. (French edition, under title *La Vie du Bouddha,* Paris, Editions Payot, 1949.)

Hamilton, Clarence. *Buddhism in India, Ceylon, China, and Japan.* University of Chicago Press, 1931.
Reading guide and general outline of Buddhist sects, scriptures, etc.

Keith, Arthur Berriedale. *Buddhist Philosophy in India and Ceylon.* Oxford, Clarendon Press, 1923.
This is probably the best single-volume analysis of Theravāda philosophy.

Oldenberg, Hermann. *Buddha; His Life, His Doctrine, His Order,* tr. from the German by William Hoey. London, Williams and Norgate, 1882; Calcutta, Book Co., 1927; London, Luzac, 1928.
An early account of Theravada Buddhism, but still one of the best and most authoritative.

Rhys-Davids, Thomas William. *Buddhism: Its History and Literature.* 3d ed. rev. New York and London, Putnam, 1896.
A standard but somewhat outdated discussion of Theravāda Buddhism.

Thomas, Edward J. *The History of Buddhist Thought.* 1st ed., London, Kegan Paul, Trench, Trubner, 1933; New York, Knopf, 1933; 2d ed., New York, Barnes and Noble, 1951; London, Routledge and Kegan Paul, 1951.
A good survey of the development of Buddhist thought from the earliest schools through Mahāyāna religion and philosophy.

——— *The Life of Buddha as Legend and History.* 1st ed., New York, Knopf, 1927; London, Kegan Paul, 1927; 3d ed., New York, Barnes and Noble, 1952.
  Study of the historical and literary evidence pertinent to the life of the Buddha.

Weiler, Royal. "The Buddhist Act of Compassion," in Ernest Bender, ed., *Indological Studies in Honor of W. Norman Brown.* New Haven, American Oriental Society, 1962.

Winternitz, Moriz. *A History of Indian Literature.* (See above, under General Works, for full bibliographical information.) Vol. II, pp. 1-226.
  The best survey of Buddhist texts and literature. Mahāyāna materials are also included.

TOPICS FOR DISCUSSION

1. The Buddha as a religious teacher, philosopher, mystic, prophet, or savior. His life in the Indian context.
2. The Four Aryan or "Noble" Truths and the Eightfold Path as a diagnosis of the universal human predicament and as a prescription for it.
3. The silence of the Buddha: types of questions that the Buddha considered irrelevant to the problem of suffering.
4. The doctrine of Dependent Origination as an answer to such questions as the creation of the world, the origin of suffering, and general causation.
5. Ethics and an individualistic approach to life through meditation and self-mastery.
6. The role of monasticism in Buddhism: the individual mendicant and the organization of the monks.
7. Should Buddhism be considered pessimistic in view of its concepts of karma, rebirth, no-soul, the evanescence of life, and the extinction of desire (*nirvāna*)?
8. Is *nirvāna* an object of desire?

THERAVĀDA BUDDHISM:
THE DHAMMAPADA (*ca.* 300 B.C.)

A short work of 423 verses dealing with central themes of Buddhism, perhaps the most popular and influential Buddhist text.

TRANSLATIONS

Babbitt, Irving. *The Dhammapada.* New York and London, Oxford University Press, 1936.
A literary but inaccurate rendition, accompanied by an essay on Buddha and the Occident.
Max Müller, Friedrich. *The Dhammapada, A Collection of Verses.* (Sacred Books of the East, vol. 10.) Oxford, Clarendon Press, 1881.
Probably the best translation, but somewhat outdated. This translation is reproduced in Lin Yutang, *The Wisdom of China and India* (New York, Random House, 1942), pp. 321-56; Clarence Hamilton, *Buddhism* (New York, Liberal Arts Press, 1952), pp. 64-97; and E. Wilson, *Sacred Books of the East* (New York, Willey Book Co., 1945), pp. 113-51.
Nārada Thera. *The Dhammapada.* London, John Murray, 1954.
A good translation by a Buddhist monk, with copious notes of a religious or philosophical rather than philological nature.
Radhakrishnan, Sarvepalli. *The Dhammapada.* London, Oxford University Press, 1950.
A good translation, partially guided by Max Müller's, with an illuminating introductory essay. This translation is reproduced, almost completely, in Radhakrishnan and Charles

A. Moore, eds., *A Source Book in Indian Philosophy*, (London, Oxford University Press, 1957; Princeton University Press, 1957), pp. 292-325.

SECONDARY READINGS

Beal, Samuel. *A Catena of Buddhist Scriptures from the Chinese.* London, Trubner, 1871; pp. 188-203.
———— *Texts from the Buddhist Canon, Commonly Known as Dhammapada, with Accompanying Narrative.* Boston, Houghton, 1878; London, Kegan Paul, Trench, Trübner, 1878; 2d ed., London, Kegan Paul, Trench, Trübner, 1902; reprint, Calcutta, Gupta, 1952.
Brough, John. *The Gāndāra Dharmapada.* London, Oxford University Press, 1962.
Burlingame, Eugene W. *Buddhist Legends.* (Harvard Oriental Series, vols. 28-30.) Cambridge, Harvard University Press, 1921; London, Oxford University Press, 1922.
The traditional commentary on the *Dhammapada*, primarily a compilation of Buddhist legends and tales meant to illustrate the application and occasion for the Buddha's preaching the verses of the *Dhammapada*. Ascribed to Buddhaghosa.
Fausset, Hugh l'Anson. "Thoughts on the Dhammapada," in *Poets and Pundits: A Collection of Essays.* London, Cape, 1947; New Haven, Yale University Press, 1949; pp. 262-69.

TOPICS FOR DISCUSSION

1. The *Dhammapada* as wisdom literature: its poetic form and imagery.
2. The focus on the individual man and his moral cultivation.
3. Moral behavior as a way of dealing with suffering.
4. Interpretation of traditional concepts, such as the Self (*ātman*), the Brahman-priest (*brāhmaṇa*), and mind or

thought (*citta*), in moral terms.
5. The relation of *nirvāṇa* to thought, pleasure, and happiness.

THERAVĀDA BUDDHISM:
THE MILINDAPAÑHĀ (*ca.* 1st cent. A.D.)

*One of the most important paracanonical prose works of
Theravāda Buddhism. A dialogue between a Greek king,
Milinda (Menander), and a Buddhist monk, Nāgasena.*

TRANSLATIONS

Horner, I. B. *King Milinda's Questions (Milindapañha).*
(Sacred Books of the Buddhists, vols. 22 and 23.) Vol. I.
London, Luzac, 1963.
Rhys-Davids, Thomas William. *The Qestions of King Milinda.*
(Sacred Books of the East, vols. 35, 36.) Oxford, Clarendon
Press, 1890-94. (Reprinted, New York, Dover, 1963.)
A fine translation by a competent scholar.

SECONDARY READINGS

Rhys-Davids, Caroline A. F. *The Milinda-Questions: An
Inquiry into Its Place in the History of Buddhism.* London,
George Routledge, 1930.
A scholarly study of the text with several original ideas
regarding its composition, authorship, and interpretation.
Winternitz, Moriz. *A History of Indian Literature.* (See above,
under General Works, for full bibliographical information.)
Vol. II, pp. 174-83.
An excellent account of the work with emphasis on its
composition and literary qualities.

TOPICS FOR DISCUSSION

1. What is the aim of the work? To what kind of audience is it addressed?
2. The composite nature of man and the doctrine of non-self.
3. If there is no transmigration, what is the nature of rebirth?
4. The relation of wisdom, faith, perseverance, mindfulness, and meditation to the attainment of *nirvāṇa*.
5. The Chain of Causation: ignorance, "confections," phenomenal being, suffering.
6. Problems and dilemmas:
   a. Why should a perfectly enlightened person, such as the Buddha, suffer and die?
   b. What is meant by Truth? What is an Act of Truth? How is this understanding related to the resolution of textual contradictions?
   c. What is wrong with philosophical discussion?
   d. If life is suffering, why is suicide not a way out?
   e. Why do the virtuous suffer and the wicked prosper?
7. Reasons for joining the Buddhist Order.
8. Stylistic features of the work that contribute to the force of its argument; the use of analogy and metaphor.

THERAVĀDA BUDDHISM: THE MAHĀSATIPAṬṬHANA SUTTA

THE GREATER DISCOURSE ON THE FOUNDATIONS OF MIND-FULNESS, *one of the "larger discourses" of the Pāli canon, has long been a primary Theravāda text on the most essential of Buddhist practices—meditation.*

TRANSLATIONS

Nyanaponika Thera. *The Heart of Buddhist Meditation.* New York, Samuel Weiser, 1970.
A fine translation with perceptive commentary and a useful introduction, by a European adherent of Theravāda.
Soma Thera. *The Way of Mindfulness: The Satipaṭṭhana Sutta and Commentary.* Kandy, Ceylon, Buddhist Publication Society, 1967.
A literal translation incorporating the classical Pāli commentary.

SECONDARY READINGS

Buddhaghosa. *The Path of Purification (Visuddhimagga),* tr. Bhikkhu Nyanamoli. Colombo, Gunasena, 1964.
The "Summa" of Theravāda meditation.
Conze, Edward. *Buddhist Meditation.* London, Allen and Unwin, 1956; New York, Harper Torchbooks, 1970.
A useful collection of texts on meditation.
Dhammasudhi, Sobhana. *Insight Meditation.* 2nd ed. London, Committee for the Advancement of Buddhism, 1968.
A cogent explanation by a modern Thai meditation master.

Swearer, Donald K. *Secrets of the Lotus.* New York, Macmillan, 1971.
An original treatment of Buddhist meditation.
Upatissa. *The Path of Freedom (Vimuttimagga),* tr. Rev. N.R.M. Ehara, *et al.* Colombo, Gunasena, 1961.
A translation from the Chinese of a shorter compendium of Theravada meditation.
Vajirañāna, Paravahera Mahāthera. *Buddhist Meditation in Theory and Practice.* Colombo, Gunasena, 1962.
An authoritative modern study of Theravāda meditation, based largely on Buddhaghosa.

TOPICS FOR DISCUSSION

1. How is such a meditative practice related to the early buddhist reaching of momentariness (the theory of elements, *dhamma*)?
2. What relevance does this sutta have for the layman?
3. Is such a teaching "quietistic" or "activistic" or both?
4. How would Mahayanists have viewed the teaching of this sutta?

MAHĀYĀNA BUDDHISM: PRAJÑĀ-PĀRAMITĀ (ca. 100 B.C.—A.D. 400)

The Buddhist texts which deal with the "Perfection of Wisdom" (Prajñāpāramitā) are among the earliest of Mahāyāna scriptures. They are the foundation of much later Buddhist thought and are especially associated with Nāgārjuna, one of India's greatest thinkers and founder of the Mādhyamika or "Middle Way" tradition. Despite their extraordinary influence on scholastic Buddhism, however, these texts are regarded by their adherents as scriptures rather than philosophical treatises.

TRANSLATIONS

The term "Prajñāpāramitā" refers to a class of texts of varying length. For a detailed survey of the literature see Edward Conze, THE PRAJÑĀPĀRAMITĀ LITERATURE (The Hague, Mouton, 1960). Cf. Moriz Winternitz, A HISTORY OF INDIAN LITERATURE (for full bibliographical information, see above under General Works), Vol. II, pp. 313-24 passim. For short selections, see the various anthologies cited under Theravāda Buddhism, above.

Conze, Edward. *Aṣṭasāhasrikā Prajñāpāramitā.* Calcutta, Asiatic Society, 1958.
An excellent translation of one of the oldest Prajñāpāramitā texts by a specialist on the subject.
────── *Buddhist Wisdom Books: Containing the Diamond Sutra and the Heart Sutra.* London, Allen and Unwin, 1958.
Includes the "Heart" sūtra with the Sanskrit text and translator's commentary.

—— *The Large Sutra on Perfect Wisdom, with the Divisions of the Abhi Samayalankara.* London, Luzac, 1961.

—— *Selected Sayings from the Perfection of Wisdom.* London, Buddhist Society, 1955.

This volume of texts is probably the most useful introduction to this somewhat obscure literature.

——. *Vajracchedika Prajñāpāramitā.* (Serie orientale Roma, vol. 13.) Rome, Instituto Italiano per il Medio ed Estremo Oriente, 1957.

A critical edition of the text with translation, introduction, and glossary.

Max Müller, Friedrich. *Buddhist Mahayana Texts.* (Sacred Books of the East, vol. 49.) London, Oxford University Press, 1894.

This useful volume includes, in addition to the "Diamond" and "Heart" sūtras, the classic life of the Buddha *(Buddhacarita)* of Aśvaghosa and the larger and smaller *Sukhavativyūha* texts.

Suzuki, D. T. *Manual of Zen Buddhism.* New York, Grove Press, 1960.

Contains translations from the Chinese of both the "Diamond" and "Heart" sūtras.

Thomas, Edward J. *The Perfection of Wisdom. The Career of the Predestined Buddhas: A Selection of Mahāyāna Scriptures.* London, John Murray, 1952.

Competent translation of Mahāyāna Buddhist texts which illustrate through parable and doctrine the superiority of Mahāyāna and the ideal of the Bodhisattva.

SECONDARY READINGS

See also Theravāda Buddhism, above.

Conze, Edward. "The Ontology of the Prajñāpāramitā," *Philosophy East and West,* III, no. 2 (July, 1953), 117-29.

A useful discussion of the metaphysical concepts of the

Prajñāpāramitā texts, especially *dharmas* and emptiness, as well as psychological and religious factors.
———— *Thirty Years of Buddhist Studies*. Oxford, Cassirer, 1967.
A collection of several useful articles on Prajñāpāramitā and related topics by the expert in the field.

Murti, T. R. V. *The Central Philosophy of Buddhism: A Study of the Mādhyamika System*. London, Allen and Unwin, 1955.
A critical and comparative study of the *Mādhyamika* system of Mahāyāna Buddhist philosophy which derives from the Prajñāpāramitā texts.

Obermiller, Eugene. "A Study of the Twenty Aspects of *Śūnyatā* (Based on Haribhadra's *Abhisamayālamkārālokā* and the *Pañcaviṃśatisāhasrikā-prajñāpāramitāsūtra*)," *Indian Historical Quarterly*, IX (1933), 170-87.
———— "The Term *Śūnyatā* in Its Different Interpretations," *Journal of Greater India Society*, I (1934), 105-17.

Robinson, Richard H. *Early Mādhyamika in India and China*. Madison, University of Wisconsin Press, 1967; pp. 1-70.
A systematic presentation of Nāgārjuna's thought using techniques of analysis derived from modern logic and linguistic philosophy.

Streng, Frederick J. *Emptiness: A Study in Religious Meaning*. New York, Abingdon Press, 1967.
An illuminating study of Nāgārjuna's use of the term *śūnya* (empty or void) which is basic Prajñāpāramitā. Streng treats the topic, in terms of modern philosophy, as a case study in the uses of religious language. He includes translations of two of Nāgārjuna's basic works and an exhaustive bibliography.

Suzuki, D. T. "The Philosophy and Religion of the Prajñāpāramitā," in *Essays in Zen Buddhism*, Third Series. London, Luzac, 1934; pp. 207-88.
A treatment of the religious and devotional aspects of the Perfection of Wisdom.

TOPICS FOR DISCUSSION

1. A fundamentally negative method, constituting a *via negativa* to Perfect Wisdom *(prajñā)*.
2. The ineffability of Perfect Wisdom.
3. Emptiness *(śūnyatā)* as a basis for enlightenment; enlightenment as "suchness."
4. Ethical implications of compassion and "skill in means."
5. The perfection of virtues, especially Wisdom *(prajñā)*, in the person of the Bodhisattva.
6. The relation of the Bodhisattva to the Buddha: the Perfection of Wisdom *(prajñāpāramitā)* and enlightenment as immanent and transcendent. The Bodhisattva as manifesting the immanence of the Perfection of Wisdom, and the Buddha as representing the transcendence of enlightenment.

MAHĀYĀNA BUDDHISM: THE ŚRĪ-MĀLĀDEVISIMHANĀDA SŪTRA

The Lion's Roar of Queen Śrīmāla *is a basic Mahāyāna sūtra containing many of the common Mahāyāna teachings, but devoted especially to the notion of the Tathāgatagarbha or "Embryo of the Tathāgata"—Buddhism's most compelling metaphor for the immanence of absolute truth. This sūtra also attests to the theoretically prominent status of lay persons within Mahāyāna.*

TRANSLATIONS

Wayman, Alex and Hideko. *The Lion's Roar of Queen Śrīmāla.* New York, Columbia University Press, 1973.
A translation based on the Tibetan and Chinese texts, extensively annotated and with a long, informative introduction.

SECONDARY READINGS

Ruegg, David Seyfort. *La théorie du tathāgatagarbha et du gotra: études sur la sotériologie et la gnoséologie du Bouddhisme.* Publications de l'École Française d'Extrême-Orient, LXX. Paris, École Française d'Extrême-Orient, 1969; pp. 30-70, 245-408.
Suzuki, D. T. *Outlines of Mahāyāna Buddhism.* New York, Schocken Books, 1963.
A broad, interpretative introduction to Mahāyāna which places Tathāgatagarbha theory in its Mahāyāna context.

TOPICS FOR DISCUSSION

1. To what extent does the theory of Perfections—giving, etc.—apply to the layman?
2. What is the difference between the Dharmakāya and the Tathāgatagarbha?
3. The *Śrīmālā* as inspired utterance.
4. How does the saint (arahat) fare in the theory of the "One Vehicle?"
5. What is the *Śrīmālā*'s teaching concerning faith?

MAHĀYĀNA BUDDHISM: THE LAŃ-KĀVATĀRA SŪTRA

The Sūtra of the Descent into Laṅka (Ceylon) *is a rich but amorphous mixture of general Mahāyāna themes and discussions of the dynamics of consciousness. Its emphasis on interior experience testifies to the continuing importance of meditation in Mahāyāna Buddhism, while its "mind-only" teachings anticipate the "idealism" of the Yogācara tradition of Mahāyāna.*

TRANSLATIONS

Suzuki, D. T. *The Laṅkāvatāra Sūtra: A Mahāyāna Text.*
London, Routledge and Kegan Paul, 1932.
An excellent translation of a very difficult text, based on the Sanskrit, Tibetan, and Chinese versions.

SECONDARY READINGS

Suzuki, D. T. *Studies in the Laṅkāvatāra Sūtra.* London, Routledge and Kegan Paul, 1930.
A companion volume to Suzuki's translation and by far the most informative and authoritative treatment of the text.
Thomas, Edward J. *The History of Buddhist Thought.* London, Routledge and Kegan Paul, 1951; pp. 230-48.
See also the relevant chapters in surveys of Indian Buddhism listed under *Supplementary Readings on Indian Buddhism.*

TOPICS FOR DISCUSSION

1. The relationship between the seventh consciousness (*manas*) and the eighth consciousness, the storehouse consciousness (*ālayavijñāna*).
2. The *Laṅkāvatarā* as a map prepared by meditators and their systematizers.
3. In "turning over" or "revulsion" (*parāvritti*), what turns over? What does it become?
4. Does the storehouse consciousness in any way resemble the "Self" of Brahmanism?
5. The storehouse consciousness and the unconscious of psychoanalysis.

MAHĀYĀNA BUDDHISM:
THE SUKHAVATIVYŪHA SŪTRAS

The longer and shorter SUKHAVATIVYŪHA SŪTRAS *concern the vision of Amitābha Buddha's "Land of Bliss" (Sukhavati), the Western Paradise. They are especially representative of the devotional aspects of Mahāyāna and yet they have their roots in Buddhist meditation. Together they bear eloquently affective witness to the universality of a spiritual tradition which promises salvation even to those who are incapable of the intellectual or meditative rigors of other strains in Mahāyāna.*

TRANSLATIONS

Cowell, E. B., *et al. Buddhist Mahāyāna Texts.* Sacred Books of the East, 49. Oxford, Clarendon Press, 1890; Repr. New Delhi, Motilal Banarsidass, 1968, and New York, Dover Paperbacks, 1969.
Includes both the larger and smaller *Sukhavativyūha Sūtras* with a useful introduction.
Shinshu Seiten. Honolulu, Higashi Honpa Hongwanji, 1955; repr. 1961; pp. 7-106.
Both sūtras are regarded as scriptural authorities in the Pure Land tradition of Japanese Buddhism and are thus included in this standard edition of the True Pure Land Sect's canon. The translations are from the Chinese versions which differ only slightly from the Sanskrit.

SECONDARY READINGS

Consult the relevant chapters in surveys of Indian Buddhism listed under *Supplementary Readings on Indian*

Buddhism and the works on Pure Land Buddhism listed under *Supplementary Readings on Japanese Buddhism.*

TOPICS FOR DISCUSSION

1. Is faith alone sufficient for rebirth into the Land of Bliss? What is the place of repentance, good conduct, and meditation on Amitābha and his Land?
2. The delights of the Land of Bliss as an aid in reaching enlightenment (*bodhi*) rather than as an end in themselves.
3. The extremely lush, pictorial style of these sūtras.
4. What is Śākyamuni's place in the drama of Amitābha?
5. The teaching of rebirth into the Land of Bliss as an expedient (*upāya*).

MAHĀYĀNA BUDDHISM: THE BODHICARYĀVATĀRA OF SHĀNTIDEVA (*ca.* A.D. 650)

This primarily devotional work occupies a position in Mahāyāna Buddhism analogous to those of the BHAGAVADGĪ-TĀ *in Hinduism, the* DHAMMAPADA *in Theravāda Buddhism, and the* IMITATIO CHRISTI *of Thomas á Kempis in Christianity.*

TRANSLATIONS

Barnett, Lionel D. *The Path of Light.* London, John Murray, 1909; New York, Dutton, 1909; 2d ed., London, John Murray, 1947; New York, Grove Press, 1948.
  A good translation of about two thirds of the text, omitting, however, the important philosophical concepts of the ninth chapter.
Conze, Edward. *Buddhist Meditation.* London, Allen and Unwin, 1956; New York, Macmillan, 1956.
  Translation of only a very few verses.
Finot, Louis. *La marche à la lumière.* (Les Classiques de l'Orient, 2.) Paris, Éditions Bossard, 1920.
  One of the best complete translations to date in a Western language.
La Vallée Poussin, L. de. *Introduction à la pratique des futurs Bouddhas, poème de Çāntideva.* Paris, Bloud, 1907.
  An excellent French translation by an outstanding authority on Buddhism.
Matics, Marion L. *Entering the Path of Enlightenment: The*

Bodhicaryāvatāra of the Buddhist Poet Śāntideva. New York, Macmillan, 1970.
The first complete English translation, preceded by a long and useful introduction.

Schmidt, Richard. *Der Eintritt in den Wandel in Erleuchtung.* Paderborn, Ferdinance Schöningh, 1923.
An excellent German translation.

SECONDARY READINGS

Bendall, Cecil, and W. H. D. Rouse. *Śikshā-samuccaya; A Compendium of Buddhist Doctrine.* London, John Murray, 1922.
A fine translation of Shāntideva's longer work: an anthology, with comment, of Mahāyāna texts. The metrical epitome in twenty-seven stanzas of this "Compendium of Instruction" is provided by L. D. Barnett, *The Path of Light,* pp. 103-7.

Dayal, Har. *The Bodhisattva Doctrine in Buddhist Sanskrit Literature.* London, Routledge, 1931. Repr. New Delhi, Motilal Banardidass, 1970.
Probably the best critical study of the textual evidence dealing with the career of the Bodhisattva.

Dutt, Nalinaksha. *Aspects of Mahāyāna Buddhism and Its Relation to Hīnayāna.* London, Luzac, 1930.

Thomas, Edward J. *The Quest of Enlightenment: A Selection of the Buddhist Scriptures.* London, John Murray, 1950.
A short anthology of Mahāyāna texts in translation with particular reference to the career of the Bodhisattva.

Winternitz, Moriz. *A History of Indian Literature.* (See above, under General Works, for full bibliographical information.) Vol. II, 370-74.
Short summary of the work.

TOPICS FOR DISCUSSION

1. The Thought of Enlightenment (*bodhicitta*): its nature and attainment. What significance does it have in a philosophy based on Emptiness (*śūnyatā*)?
2. The Bodhisattva as the ideal man.
3. The Perfection of the virtues of patience or long suffering (*kṣānti*), courage (*vīrya*), and meditation (*dhyāna*), and their application to a world conceived as suffering.
4. The Perfection of Wisdom (*prajñāpāramitā*) as a philosophical basis for piety.
5. The Buddhist concept of compassion: its relation to the Bodhisattva's vow and the concept of Truth.
6. Conquest of evil through pious meditation and moral action.

SUPPLEMENTARY READINGS ON INDIAN BUDDHISM

Readers may wish to consult anthologies, surveys, and histories of Indian Buddhism. Among these the following should prove useful.

Bareau, André. *Bouddhisme*. Les religions de l'Inde, III. Paris, Payot, 1966.
One of the best and most clearly organized short surveys.
Berry, Thomas. *Buddhism*. New York, Hawthorn Books, 1966.
A perceptive overview of the entire Buddhist tradition.
Conze, Edward, *et al. Buddhist Texts Through the Ages*. London, Cassirer, 1954; repr. New York, Harper Torchbooks, 1964.
A fine selection of brief texts from all of Buddhism's canonical languages.
───── *Buddhist Thought in India*. London, Allen and Unwin, 1962; Ann Arbor, Univ. of Michigan Press, 1967.
Especially good on Buddhist scholasticism.
De Bary, Wm. Theodore, *et al. The Buddhist Tradition in India, China, and Japan*. New York, The Modern Library, 1969.
The first third of this comprehensive anthology includes a judicious selection of well translated texts from both the Theravāda and Mahāyāna traditions.
Dutt, Sukumar. *Buddhist Monks and Monasteries of India*. London, Allen and Unwin, 1962.
A good survey of the institutional development of Indian Buddhism.

Jayatilleke, K. N. *Early Buddhist Theory of Knowledge.* London, Allen and Unwin, 1963. Not nearly so narrow in scope as its title suggests.

Lamotte, Étienne. *Histoire du Bouddhisme indien, des origines à l'ère Śaka.* Louvain, Publications Universitaries, 1958. The most thorough and comprehensive history of Indian Buddhism, a monument of scholarship.

Rahula, Walpola. *What the Buddha Taught.* New York, Grove Press, 1962.

Robinson, Richard H. *The Buddhist Religion.* Belmont, California, Dickenson, 1970. An excellent brief survey of the entire tradition, more than two-thirds of which is devoted to India.

Saddhatissa, H. *The Buddha's Way.* New York, George Braziller, 1971.

Sangharakshita, Bhikshu. *A Survey of Buddhism.* Bangalore, The Indian Institute of World Culture, 1959.

Warder, A. K. *Indian Buddhism.* Delihi, Motilal Banardidass, 1970. One of the best surveys of all of Indian Buddhism in English.

Wayman, Alex. "Buddhism," in C. J. Bleeker and G. Widengren, eds. *Historia Religionum, II, Religions of the Present.* Leiden, E. J. Brill, 1972. An excellent survey, arranged topically rather than chronologically.

SHAKUNTALĀ (ABHIJÑĀNAŚAKUN-
TALĀ) OF KĀLIDĀSA (ca. A.D. 400)

SHAKUNTALĀ is the major drama of Kālidāsa, the greatest of Indian dramatists.

TRANSLATIONS

Das Gupta, Kedar Nath. *Sakuntala, by Kalidasa,* prepared for the English stage by Kedar Nath Das Gupta in a new version edited by Lawrence Binyon. London, Macmillan, 1920. A much adapted version with particular emphasis on the use of the play for the English stage. There is a stimulating essay by Rabindranath Tagore.

Emeneau, M. B. *Abhijñāna-śakuntalā.* Berkeley, University of California Press (paperback), 1962. An accurate literal translation from the Bengali (longer) recension.

Kale, M. R. *The Abhijnāśakuntalā of Kālidāsa.* Bombay, 1961. (1st ed., 1898.) Good introduction, text, and commentary.

Lal, P. *Great Sanskrit Plays in Modern Translation.* Norfolk, Conn., New Directions (clothbound and paperback eds.), 1964. Translations of six plays, including *Shakuntalā,* in vigorous English, by an Indian poet. There is a very useful introduction to Sanskrit drama in general, and a briefer one for each play. The translator has striven to recreate the effect of the Sanskrit play rather than to give a literal translation.

Monier-Williams, M. *Śakuntalā.* Hertford, Madden, 1853; 2d

ed., Oxford, Clarendon Press, 1876.
A critical translation of all metrical passages from the Devanagari (shorter) recension of the text.
——— *Śakoontalā; or, The Lost Ring.* Hertford, Madden, 1855; New York, Dodd, Mead, 1885; 5th ed., London, John Murray, 1887.
A very competent translation of the Devanāgarī, or shorter, recension of the drama, also available in an inexpensive anthology (John D. Yohannan, *A Treasury of Asian Literature* [New York, New American Library (Mentor), 1960], pp. 131-272).

Ryder, Arthur W. *Kalidasa: Translations of Shakuntala and Other Works.* New York, Dutton, 1912; London, Dent, 1912. Also under title *Shakuntala and Other Writings by Kalidasa.* New York, Dutton (Everyman paperback), 1959.
Translation of the drama from the Bengali recension. The translation of the verse portions, while accurate, does not always preserve the dignified quality of the original text.

SECONDARY READINGS

Emeneau, M. B. "Kālidāsa's Śakuntalā and the Mahābhārata," *Journal of the American Oriental Society,* LXXXII, no. 1 (March, 1962), 41-44.
An attempt to prove that Kālidāsa relied on the *Mahābhārata* for the story version of *Shakuntalā* rather than on the *Padma Purāṇa,* as maintained by Winternitz and Sarma.
Harris, Mary B. *Kalidasa, Poet of Nature.* Boston, Meador Press, 1936.
A general discussion of Kālidāsa's treatment of nature, animal life, etc.
Hillebrandt, Alfred. *Kālidāsa: Ein Versuch zu seiner literarischen Würdigung.* Breslau, Marcus, 1921.
An excellent scholarly study of the poet and his works, life, times, sources, etc., as well as his talent as an artist, humorist, and philosopher.

Jhala, G. C. *Kālidāsa, a Study.* Bombay, Padma Publications, 1943.

A study of the poet-dramatist and his works. *Shakuntalā* is discussed (pp. 130-59) in terms of the author's literary improvements of an old story. This book also contains a statement on Kālidāsa's conception of love (pp. 160-74).

Keith, Arthur Berriedale. *The Sanskrit Drama: Its Origin, Development, Theory and Practice.* Oxford, Clarendon Press, 1924; pp. 152-67.

Includes a summary of the play and remarks on Kālidāsa's dramatic art, style, language, and meters.

Levi, Sylvain. *Le Théâtre indien.* Paris, Bouillon, 1890.

A classical treatment of the Indian theater by an outstanding Indic scholar.

Misra, Vidya Niwas. "The Mango-Blossom Imagery in Kālidāsa," *Journal of the American Oriental Society,* LXXXII, no. 1 (March, 1962), 68-69.

A short note on the mango-blossom as an object of nature, an emblem of fruitful love, and a symbol of womanhood, in Kālidāsa's poems and the drama, *Shakuntalā.*

Mitchell, John D. "A Sanskrit Classic: Shakuntalā," in Wm. Theodore de Bary, ed., *Approaches to the Oriental Classics.* New York, Columbia University Press, 1959; pp. 119-31. With comments by Royal W. Weiler, pp. 132-36.

A primarily psychological study of the play and its characters, although the levels of "immediate appeal" (as a theater-piece) and cultural significance are also treated. The comments point out the universal characteristics of this drama, and give some indication of available literature and translations.

Raghavan, V. *Love in the Poems and Plays of Kālidāsa.* Bangalore, Indian Institute of Culture, 1954.

Accurate translation by a leading Indian scholar.

Wells, Henry Willis. *The Classical Drama of India: Studies in Its Value for the Literature and Theatre of the World.* Bombay, Asia Publishing House, 1963.

TOPICS FOR DISCUSSION

1. The stylization of characters: hero, heroine, *vidushaka*, *vita*. Which of the persons of the drama really have character? How is characterization achieved? Can this be related to anything in the religious or philosophical background of India?

2. The understanding of "love" in the plays. The attempt to create a mood of tenderness, of girl's first love. The varieties of love.

3. The audience and the structure of the play.

4. Attitude to nature as "human."

5. Tragedy in the Indian drama: characters move in a just and understandable world; no mysteries or ambiguities; destiny is made by man, not something against which he struggles.

6. Does the drama have any of the overtones of a parable or allegory? What is the significance of Shakuntala's background?

7. Does one have any sense of participation in the drama through identification with any of the characters?

8. Specifically "traditional" notes: Brahman's curse; caste; obedience to parents; wife's duty to husband.

9. The reason for the use of poetry.

10. Use of signs and symbols: throbbing arm, vine and mango, black bee, etc.

11. Two levels of working out of karma. Cf. with *Rāmāyana*.

THE LITTLE CLAY CART (MRCCHAKATIKĀ) OF SHŪDRAKA (*ca.* A.D. 400)

THE LITTLE CLAY CART, *attributed to King Shūdraka, is the Indian drama most frequently adapted for Western audiences.*

TRANSLATIONS

Lal, P. *Great Sanskrit Plays in Modern Translation.* Norfolk, Conn., New Directions (clothbound and paperback eds.), 1964.
Includes a translation of *The Little Clay Cart* under the title *The Toy Cart.* For further annotation, see under *Shakuntalā.*

Oliver, Revilo Pendleton. *Mrcchakatikā, the Little Clay Cart.* Urbana, University of Illinois Press, 1938.
A careful and meticulous translation with copious notes, an excellent introduction, and helpful appendices discussing the Indian context of the play.

Ryder, Arthur W. *The Little Clay Cart (Mrcchakatikā).* (Harvard Oriental Series, vol. 9.) Cambridge, Harvard University Press, 1905.
An accurate, highly literary translation, which attmpts to reproduce many of the stylistic nuances of the original.

Van Buitenen, J. A. B. *Two Plays of Ancient India: The Little Clay Cart and The Minister's Seal.* New York, Columbia University Press, 1968.
Lively, scholarly English translations, enhanced by an excellent introduction to Indian drama.

Wilson, Horace Hayman. *The Mrichchhakati, or, The Toy*

Cart. Calcutta, V. Holcroft, 1826. Reprint, with additional material, in *Hindu Dramatic Works.* Calcutta, Society for the Resuscitation of Indian Literature, 1901.

―――― Same [excerpts], in *Select Specimens of the Theatre of the Hindus.* London, Parbury Allen, 1828; 3d ed., London, Trübner, 1871. Reprint, with additional material, under title *The Theatre of the Hindus.* Calcutta, Gupta, 1955.
Much outdated but still interesting translations.

SECONDARY READINGS

Bhat, G. K. *Preface to Mrcchakatikā.* Ahmedabad, New Order Book Co., 1953.
A critical study of this drama with special attention given to plot construction, characterizatipn, humor, and background.

Faddegon, B. "Mrcchakatikā and King Lear," in *India Antiqua; A Volume of Oriental Studies.* Leiden, Brill, 1947; pp. 113-23.
A provocative article by an excellent Indic scholar.

Keith, Arthur Berriedale. *The Sanskrit Drama: Its Origin, Development, Theory and Practice.* Oxford, Clarendon Press, 1924; pp. 128-42.
A short account of the story, the authorship and age of the work, and the language and meters.

TOPICS FOR DISCUSSION

(Cf. topics under SHAKUNTALĀ, *most of which are pertinent here.)*
  1. The cosmopolitan qualities of the drama: the minimal use of strictly Hindu imagery, theme, and symbol, and the greater appeal of the work to Western audiences.
  2. The structure of the play: the interweaving of plots. Could any of them be deleted without loss to the play?

3. The characterizations and the expression of human emotions. Cārudatta as a real hero; Vasantasenā, a courtesan, as a real heroine, and Sansthānaka, the parasite (*viṭa*), as a villain. Maitreya's role as a confidant (*vidūṣaka*).

4. The intricacy of the plot: a main plot with several subplots (Sharvilaka and Madanikā; the political revolt) carefully interwoven to create a sense of unity.

5. Didactic elements: the use of moral maxims and clichés as dramatic devices.

6. The expression of Indian humor and the question of satire in this drama.

7. Buddhist elements: compassion, charity, karma, realism (as opposed to the ephemeral atmosphere of *Shakuntalā*), a monk, and urban setting.

PAÑCATANTRA (ca. 200 B.C.).
ACCORDING TO PŪRṆABHADRA
(ca. A.D. 1199)

This collection of ancient Indian fables has exerted a greater influence on world literature than any other Indian work. It has been called the best collection of stories in the world.

TRANSLATIONS

a. COMPLETE

Edgerton, Franklin. *The Panchatantra Reconstructed.* (American Oriental Series, vol. 3.) New Haven, Conn., American Oriental Society, 1924.
An excellent translation of the reconstructed original text of the *Pañcatantra.* The translation is marred only by the author's idiosyncrasy in spelling. The volume includes a useful introduction discussing the origin, composition, and migration of the fables.

Hertel, Johannes. *Tantrākhyāyika, die älteste Fassung des Pañcatantra.* Leipzig, Teubner, 1909; Berlin, Weidmann, 1910.
A fine German translation of the oldest version of the *Pañcatantra.* The first part of this volume discusses the text.

Ryder, Arthur W. *The Pañcatantra.* University of Chicago Press, 1925, reprint, 1956; Cambridge University Press, 1925, reprint, 1956; Bombay, Jaico Books. Paperback ed. University of Chicago Press (Phoenix).
A readable and accurate translation with verse portions rendered in rhyme. The best translation in English of this work.

b. SELECTIONS

Lin Yutang. *The Wisdom of China and India.* New York, Random House, 1942; pp. 265-99. (For other editions, see under *Rāmāyana.*) Excerpts from Ryder's translation of about eighteen of the most famous stories. Unfortunately, some of the verse portions of these tales have been eliminated.

Yohannan, John D. *A Treasury of Asian Literature.* New York, John Day, 1956; London, Phoenix House, 1958; New York, New American Library (Mentor), 1960, pp. 15-20. A translation of four short didactic fables by Charles R. Lanman.

SECONDARY READINGS

De, S. K. *A History of Sanskrit Literature.* University of Calcutta, 1947; pp. 86-92. A brief general statement of the *Pañcatantra,* its composition, and recensions.

Keith, Arthur Berriedale. *A History of Sanskrit Literature.* Oxford, Clarendon Press, 1928; pp. 242-65. An excellent short account and analysis of the origin of fable literature in India, the subject matter of the *Pañcatantra,* and its style and language. A short note on the genetically related *Hitopadeśa* is also included.

RELATED READINGS

Ryder, Arthur W. *Dandin: The Ten Princes.* Chicago, University of Chicago Press, 1927.

Tawney, C. H. *The Ocean of Story.* (A translation of Somadeva's *Kathāsaritsāgara.*) 10 vols. London, C. J. Sawyer, 1924-28.

Van Buitenen, J. A. B. *Tales of Ancient India.* Chicago, University of Chicago Press, 1959; paperback ed. (Phoenix), 1969.

Worthan, B. Hale. *The Enchanted Parrot*. Selections in Lin
Yutang, ed. *The Wisdom of China and India*. New York,
The Modern Library, 1942; pp. 297-318.

TOPICS FOR DISCUSSION

1. The structure of the work: boxed fables (cf. *Arabian Nights*); the function of narrative prose and verse portions.
2. The concept of and importance attached to wise moral conduct (*nīti*) in social and political relationships.
3. The use of didactic verse and moral maxims to justify or validate an action. Epigrammatic authority as a substitute for reason.
4. Worldly success and the problems of everyday life: security vs. poverty. Wit as means to resolve problems. The place of scholarship in human life. Human emotions and sentimentality.
5. The role of fate and the importance of human effort. The folly of hasty action.
6. The nature and importance of friendship in the face of adversity. The group ideal as opposed to the traditional emphasis on the spiritual wisdom of the individual ascetic.
7. The *Pañcatantra* as a practical guide for kings.
8. The use of stereotyped characters (e.g., cat: hypocrisy; jackal: craftiness; heron: stupidity, etc.). The effective use of animal characters in preference to human ones.

SANSKRIT LYRIC POETRY

Miller, Barbara Stoler. *Bhartrihari: Poems.* New York, Columbia University Press, 1967.
A bilingual edition based on D. D. Kosambi's definitive edition. The verse translation is excellent.

Ryder, Arthur W. *Women's Eyes.* San Francisco, A. M. Robertson, 1917.
Eighty-five verses from various *śatakas,* plus fifteen poems from other sources, are rendered in metrical versions which have both flaws and merits. Ryder's style is best suited to the gnomic verses.

Bilhana's *Caurapañcāśikā* (Fifty Lyrics of a Thief)—a series of verses of remembered love. (*ca.* A.D. 1070–1100)

Mathers, E. Powys. *Black Marigolds* (A free interpretation of the *Chaurapañchāśikā*). Reprinted in its entirety in Mark Van Doren, *An Anthology of World Poetry.* Harcourt, Brace and Co., 1936; pp. 66-77.

Miller, Barbara Stoler. *Phantasies of a Love-thief.* New York, Columbia University Press, 1971.
A bilingual edition, including the critically edited texts of two versions of the work, an introduction, notes, and illustrations. The verse translation is excellent.

Schwebell, Gertrude Glorious. *The Secret Delights of Love by Pundit Bilhana.* New York, Peter Pauper Press, 1966.
A retranslation of a German rendering.

b. ANTHOLOGIES

Brough, John. *Poems from the Sanskrit.* Baltimore, Penguin Books, 1968.
Translations of verses from various Sanskrit sources, with an excellent introduction.

Ingalls, Daniel H. H. *An Anthology of Sanskrit Court Poetry.* Cambridge, Harvard University Press, 1965.
Almost two thousand verses from various sources, as presented in Vidyākara's "Subhāsitaratnakosa." The intro-

duction, translations, and notes all attest to Ingall's great sensitivity for Sanskrit poetry.

———— *Sanskrit Poetry from Vidyākara's Treasury.* Cambridge, Harvard University Press, 1968.
A brief version of the above, aimed at the non-Sanskritist.

SECONDARY READINGS

De, S. K. *A History of Sanskrit Literature.* Calcutta, University of Calcutta, 1947; pp. 132-34, 161-65, and 364-69.
Ingalls, Daniel H. H. Introduction to *Sanskrit Court Poetry,* see above.
Keith, Arthur Berriedale. *A History of Sanskrit Literature.* Oxford, Clarendon Press, 1928; pp. 175-190.

RELATED READING

Ramanujan, A. K., tr. *The Interior Landscape: Love Poems from a Classical Tamil Anthology.* Bloomington, Indiana University Press, 1967.
Superb translations of Tamil lyric poetry, which has much in common with this Sanskrit poetry.

TOPICS FOR DISCUSSION

1. What particular qualities of this poetry qualify it as "lyric?"
2. How are the compressed miniature molds of the poems expanded? Consider the highly inflected Sanskrit language, the extensive use of long compound words, figures of speech, conventions, and suggestive overtones of words and images. (*dhvani*).
3. The environment of the poems—what is the role of nature? What is the relation between nature and love? How are elements of poetry used to create a particular

mood or atmosphere (*rasa*)? Consider the interplay of conventions and descriptive details.(*cf. Shakuntalā* verses.)

4. What do the verses "require" of the reader? How does the educated reader enrich the poems? Is this possible through translation?

5. The themes of Sanskrit poetry. Love-in-enjoyment and love-in-separation, the seasons, the poet's plight, the world of villains and kings, the pursuit of peace and liberation.

6. Compare the aesthetic world of Sanskrit poetry with that of classical Indian painting, sculpture, and music.

GĪTAGOVINDA OF JAYADEVA (ca. 12th cent. A.D.)

"Krishna Praised in Song" is a unique operatic lyric in Sanskrit, regarded both as a great poem and as a religious work of medieval Vaishnava devotionalism.

TRANSLATIONS

a. COMPLETE

Arnold, Edwin. *The Indian Song of Songs.* 6th ed. London, Kegan Paul, Trench, Trübner, 1891 (1st ed., 1875; Bombay, Jaico, 1949).
   A fairly accurate poetical translation, slightly bowdlerized.
Keyt, George. *Gita Govinda.* Bombay, Kutub, 1947.
   One of the most beautiful and accurate of all translations from Sanskrit into English.
Rückert, Friedrich. *Gita Gowinda oder die Liebe des Krischna und der Radha.* Berlin, Schnabel, 1920.
   An excellent translation by a gifted German poet.

b. SELECTIONS

Brough, John. *Selections from Classical Sanskrit Literature.* London, Luzac, 1951; pp. 76-83.
   The most accurate translation of cantos I, X, and XII.
Yohannan, John D. *A Treasury of Asian Literature.* New York, John Day, 1956; London, Phoenix House, 1958; New York, New American Library (Mentor), 1960, pp. 274-99.
   A selection from Keyt's translation.

SECONDARY READINGS

Archer, William George. *The Loves of Krishna in Indian Painting and Poetry.* London, Allen and Unwin, 1957; New York, Macmillan, 1957; New York, Grove (Evergreen), 1958.
A very fine survey of the Krishna-Rādhā legend as reflected in Indian painting.

De, S. K. *A History of Sanskrit Literature.* University of Calcutta, 1947; pp. 388-98.
A critical evaluation of Jayadeva's poem with reference to religious influences on the work and its position in Indian literature.

Keith, Arthur Berriedale. *A History of Sanskrit Literature.* Oxford, Clarendon Press, 1928; pp. 190-98.
A short discussion of the poet and his work.

Mukerjee, Radhakamal. *The Lord of the Autumn Moons.* Bombay, Asia Publishing House, 1957.
A very good translation, with comment and introduction, of chapters 29-33 of Book X of the *Bhāgavata Purāna* on which the *Gītagovinda* of Jayadeva is based.

Vaudeville, Charlotte. "Evolution of Love-Symbolism in Bhagavatism," *Journal of the American Oriental Society,* LXXXII, no. 1 (March, 1962), 31-40.
An illuminating article on the philosophical background of devotional Hinduism. Although the references are primarily to the *Bhagavadgītā* (see above) and Tamil poetry, this is a good article on the role of devotion (*bhakti*) in the Hindu thought basic to the *Gītagovinda.*

TOPICS FOR DISCUSSION

1. The *Gītagovinda* as an erotic and religious lyric; as an epic poem; as a dramatic lyric or a pastoral drama.
2. The ornate and artificial form; its melodic quality; its sensuous descriptions and moods (*rāga*). The function of

recitative verses following each song to portray simple action.

3. The sensuous quality of Indian love songs (cf. *Shakuntalā,* above), and its dependence on form for dramatic effect.

4. The characters: Krishna (cf. *Mahābhārata, Bhagavadgītā,* above), Rādhā, and her friend (cf. *Shakuntalā*). Do their personalities emerge in the poem?

5. Why is Lord Krishna portrayed as having human passions? What is the reason for vivid imagery describing his erotic behavior?

6. The mood and atmosphere of the poem; Jayadeva's feelings for nature.

7. The *Gītagovinda* as an allegory (cf. *Song of Songs*) or mystery play, with mystical meaning expressed in terms of devotion (*bhakti*); love of the human soul, Rādhā, for a god, Krishna.

8. Are there any distinctions made between kinds of sensuality in the poem? Is there any religious element in the sexual imagery?

INDIAN DEVOTIONAL POETRY

Bhakti poetry in three representative literary traditions: Tamil and Kannada, Hindi, and Bengali.

TRANSLATIONS

a. TAMIL AND KANNADA (*ca.* A.D. 200–1000)

Hooper, J. S. M. *Hymns of the Ālvārs.* Calcutta, Association Press, 1929.
Stiff, but one of the only readable selections of this poetry.
Kingsbury, F., and G. E. Phillips. *Hymns of the Tamil Śaivite Saints.* Calcutta, Association Press, 1921 (reissued).
As in the case of the above, a stiff translation which serves as one of the only readable selections of this poetry.

b. HINDI (KABĪR, *ca.* 1440–1518; TULASĪDĀS, *ca.* 1532–1623)

Allchin, Raymond. *Tulasī Dās: Kavitāvāli.* New York, A. S. Barnes and Co., 1964.
A readable verse translation of the work of Tulasīdās' old age, in two parts, including episodes from the Rāma legend and highly personal expressions of devotion. Excellent introduction to the poet and his poetry.
Atkins, A. G. *The Rāmāyana of Tulsī Dās, with Hindi Text.* 3 vols. New Dehli, Hindustan Times, preface 1954.
While the attempt to reproduce in English verse the prosody of the original is not very successful, the translation is reasonably accurate and gives something of the devotional flavor of Tulasīdās.

Hill, W. Douglas P. *The Holy Lake of the Acts of Rāma.* Bombay, Oxford University Press, 1952. A scholarly translation with a good introduction.

Tagore, Rabindranath; assisted by Evelyn Underhill. *One Hundred Poems of Kabīr.* London, Macmillan and Co., 1961. The Bengali poet's sympathetic renderings of songs of the weaver-mystic. Introduction by Evelyn Underhill.

c. BENGALI (*ca.* A.D. 1400–1700)

Bhattacarya, Deben. *Love Songs of Chandidas: The rebel poet-priest of Bengal.* London, Allen and Unwin, 1967. Readable translations, with introduction and notes.

——— *Love Songs of Vidyapati.* London, Allen and Unwin, 1961. The Introduction is by W. G. Archer.

Dimock, Edward C., Jr., and Denise Levertov. *In Praise of Krishna: Songs from the Bengali.* Garden City, N.Y., Anchor Books, 1967. Superb translations.

SECONDARY READINGS

Archer, W. G. *The Loves of Krishna in Indian Painting and Poetry.* New York, Grove Press, 1958.

Bhandarkar, R. G. *Vaiṣṇāvism, Śaivism and Minor Religious Systems.* Strassburg, Trübner, 1913.

Burns, R. "Kabīr, Kabīrpanthīs," *Encyclopedia of Religion and Ethics,* vol. VII, pp. 632-34.

Chatterji, Suniti Kumar. *Languages and Literatures of Modern India.* Calcutta, Prakash Bhavan, 1963. Part B.

Dasgupta, S. N. *Hindu Mysticism.* New York, Ungar Paperbacks, 1959. Lecture IV.

De Bary, Wm. Theodore, ed. *Sources of the Indian Tradition.* New York, Columbia University Press, 1958; paperback ed., 2 vols., 1964; pp. 327-66.

Dimock, Edward C., Jr. *The Place of the Hidden Moon: Erotic Mysticism in Vaishnava Sahajiyā Cult of Bengal.* Chicago, University of Chicago Press, 1966.
    Includes an excellent discussion of the role of poetic imagery and esthetics in devotionalism, orthodox and heterodox.

Grierson, George A. "Bhakti-Mārga," *Encyclopedia of Religion and Ethics*, vol. II, pp. 539-51.

———— "Tulasī-Dāsa," *Encyclopedia of Religion and Ethics*, vol. XII, pp. 469-73.

Hein, Norvin. "The Rām Līla," in Milton Singer, ed., *Traditional India: Structure and Change.* American Folklore Society, 1959; pp. 73-98.
    On the role of the Rāma legend in religious festivals of northern India.

Sastri, K. A. Nilakanta. *Development of Religion in South India.* Bombay, Orient Longmans, 1963.
    See Chapter 3, "Bhakti Movements in the South."

Singer, Milton B., ed. *Krishna: Myths, Rites, and Attitudes.* Honolulu, East-West Center Press, 1966.

TOPICS FOR DISCUSSION

1. The nature of devotion (*bhakti*) in these poems. *Cf. Bhagavadgītā, Gītagovinda.* What elements are drawn from previous religious traditions? What elements are drawn from literary traditions?

2. The language of the poetry. The effects of the vernacular languages versus Sanskrit.

3. Stylistic use of hyperbole and exaggerated imagery to create moods of heightened love, wonder, and awe.

4. Resolution of the conflict between worldly life of love (*kāma*) and the duties of religion (*dharma*) by admitting intense human emotion to the sphere of religion. The

quality of love and religious duty in relation to Krishna, Rāma, Śiva, in the various poems.

5. The characters of Krishna and Rāma: *cf.* Krishna of poetry with Krishna of *Mbh.* and *BG*; *cf.* Tulasīdāsa's and Kabīr's Rāma with Vālmīki's. The significance of various aspects of these characters: as incarnate gods in the Vedantic tradition of pantheism, as personal supreme God.

6. What is the relationship between the god and his devotee? What is the effect of love suffered in separation from the beloved? *Cf. Śakuntalā,* Vālmīki's *Rāmāyana, Caurapāñcāśika, Gītagovinda.*

INDO-ISLAMIC POETRY

Poetry written in Urdu and Persian comprises a distinct genre in Indian writing. The beauty and power of this poetry has led its admirers to rank it among the world's great literary achievements.

Translations: Eighteenth and Nineteenth Century Poets

Ahmad, Aijaz, ed. *Ghazals of Ghalib.* New York, Columbia University Press, 1971.
Versions of Urdu poems of Ghālib, generally regarded as the greatest of Urdu poets, by a number of American poets, including W. S. Merwin, Adrienne Rich, and William Stafford, based on translations by Aijaz Ahmad, a Pakistani poet.

Ali, Ahmed. *The Golden Tradition: An Anthology of Urdu Poetry.* New York, Columbia University Press, 1973.
Translations, with excellent introductory essays, of the poetry of fifteen of the most important Urdu poets.

——— *Ghalib: Selected Poems.* Rome, Is.M.E.O., 1969.
Careful, sensitive translations of both Urdu and Persian poetry.

Matthews, D. J., and C. Shackle. *An Anthology of Classical Urdu Love Lyrics.* London, Oxford University Press, 1972.
Translations of representative works of twenty-two poets, with notes on prosody, grammar, and vocabulary.

Russell, Ralph, and Khurshidul Islam. *Three Mughal Poets: Mir, Sauda, Mir Hasan.* Cambridge, Harvard University Press, 1968.
Contains a valuable introductory essay on the eighteenth

century background, with translations and critical interpretations of the work of three outstanding poets.

TRANSLATIONS: SIR MUHAMMAD IQBAL (1876–1938)

The Mysteries of Selflessness (Rumūz-i-Bekhudī), tr. by A. J. Arberry. London, John Murray, 1953.

This long Persian poem is a passionate expression of the bases of an ideal Islamic society.

The Secrets of the Self (Asrār-i-Khudī), tr. by R. A. Nicholson. London, Macmillan, 1920; rev. ed., Lahore, Ashraf, 1940.

Iqbal's most famous work, this poem asserts the role of the individual over against what seemed to Iqbal to be the false emphasis of the Sufis on mystical communion with the Divine.

SECONDARY READINGS

Iqbal, Muhammad. *The Reconstruction of Religious Thought in Islam.* London, Oxford University Press, 1934; Lahore, Ashraf, 1944.

Perhaps the clearest and best statement of Iqbal's attitude toward Islam.

Malik, Hafeez, ed. *Iqbal, Poet-Philosopher of Pakistan.* New York, Columbia University Press, 1971.

Collection of essays on many aspects of Iqbal's thought.

Russell, Ralph, and Khurshid Islam, tr. *Ghalib, 1797-1869, Vol. I, Life and Letters.* Cambridge, Harvard University Press, 1969.

The second volume will contain translations of his poetry.

Sadiq, Muhammad. *A History of Urdu Literature.* London, Oxford University Press, 1964.

Comprehensive, scholarly study.

Schimmel, Annemarie. *Gabriel's Wing: A Study of the Religious Ideas of Sir Muhammad Iqbal.* Leiden, E. J. Brill, 1963.

Authoritative analysis.

Singh, Iqbal. *The Ardent Pilgrim.* London and New York, Longman's, 1951.

Well-written study of Iqbal's life and ideas.

Vahid, S. A. *Iqbal, His Art and Thought.* Lahore, Ashraf, 1944; London, John Murray, 1959.

A useful study of Iqbal's poetry and ideas.

TOPICS FOR DISCUSSION

1. The Lover and the Beloved in Urdu poetry: how are they to be understood?
2. What is the relationship between the use of conventional imagery and originality in this kind of poetry? How does adherence to a rigid convention affect poetry?
3. In the *ghazals,* is each couplet a separate poem, or are there relationships to the main setting?
4. What is the significance of urban imagery in the Urdu poets?
5. The significance of Iqbal's exaltation of the individual self.
6. His understanding of love as "the desire to assimilate, to absorb ... Love individualizes the lover as well as the beloved."
7. His rejection of nationalism as an evil.
8. The resolution of the contradiction between the self and the community.
9. The concept of the "superman" in Iqbal's poetry.

POEMS AND PLAYS OF
RABINDRANATH TAGORE (1861–1941)

The greatest literary figure of the Indian national revival in the twentieth century.

TRANSLATIONS

Collected Poems and Plays of Rabindranath Tagore. London, Macmillan, 1936; New York, Macmillan, 1937; reissued, 1952, 1956.
Many of the translations in this collection are by the author. While they are at times quite different in mood and style from the original Bengali, they indicate the poet's sensitivity to nature and his deep kinship with the traditional poetry of Bengal.

A Flight of Swans: Poems from Balākā, tr. by A. Bose. London, John Murray, 1955.
Poems written before and during the First World War.

The Herald of Spring: Poems from Mohuā, tr. by A. Bose. London, John Murray, 1957; New York, Grove Press, 1957.
This collection of love poems was written when the author was seventy-one.

The King of the Dark Chamber, tr. by the author. London, Macmillan, 1914; New York, Macmillan, 1916.
An expression in dramatic form of the concern of much of Tagore's poetry—the mystery of the relationship between God and man.

Wings of Death, tr. by A. Bose. London, John Murray, 1960.
Poems written in the last year of Tagore's life.

Chakravarty, Amiya. *A Tagore Reader.* New York and London, Macmillan, 1961.
Selections with an introduction by a close associate of Tagore.

SECONDARY READINGS

Dimock, Edward C. "Rabindranath Tagore—'The Greatest of the Bāuls of Bengal,' " *The Journal of Asian Studies,* XIX, no. 1 (1959), 33-51.
A valuable study of the sources of Tagore's inspiration and imagery.
Ghose, S. K. *The Later Poems of Tagore.* London, Asia Publishing House, 1961.
Literary criticism with a number of translations.
Kripalani, K. *Rabindranath Tagore: A Biography.* New York, Grove Press, 1962; London, Oxford University Press, 1962.
One of the best studies of the poet's life, by a close associate.
Tagore, Rabindranath. *My Reminiscences.* New York and London, Macmillan, 1917.
Gives the background of his early life.
———— *An Eastern University.* (Visva-Bharati Bulletin, No. 7.) Calcutta, Visva-Bharati Office, 1927.
The poet's views on education and his evaluation of Western culture.
Thompson, Edward J. *Rabindranath Tagore, Poet and Dramatist.* London and New York, Oxford University Press, 1926; 2d ed. rev., New York, 1948.
Many of Thompson's literary judgments can be questioned, but his translations are good and he supplies the essential information about the poet's life.

TOPICS FOR DISCUSSION

1. Tagore's relationship to his own tradition and to that of the West.

2. The pain and joy of religious experience as a theme of Tagore's poetry.

3. Tagore's emphasis on nature mysticism in contrast to customary Hindu attitudes; his concept of nature as *māyā*.

4. The significance of Tagore's imagery: drawn from the *bhakti* tradition: birds and flute music for the elusiveness of true joy; the market place, thieves, for man's blurred sense of reality; fire for self-concern and passion; the river and boats for man's loneliness and danger.

5. Time and death in Tagore's poetry.

6. The plays as expressions of ideas rather than as dramatic works; concern with the conflict between human emotion and the bonds of tradition.

7. The relation between Tagore's poetic vision and his rejection of nationalism; his understanding of the West.

8. Evaluation of Tagore as an English poet in terms of his nineteenth-century heritage.

9. Tagore's poetry as an aid in relating Indian art to Hindu metaphysical concepts; the mingling of human and divine love.

AUTOBIOGRAPHY OF MOHANDAS KARAMCHAND GANDHI (1869–1948)

TRANSLATIONS

Gandhi, Mohandas Karamchand. *An Autobiography: The Story of My Experiments with Truth*, tr. from the Gujarati by Mahadev Desai. Washington, Public Affairs Press, 1954; Boston, Beacon Press (paperback), 1957. First published under the title *The Story of My Experiments with Truth*. 2 vols. Ahmedabad, Navajivan Press, 1927-29; 2d ed., 1940; London, Phoenix Press, 1949.

Episodic in style and lacking in narrative content, this is, nevertheless, one of the world's great autobiographies, providing insights into the motivations and actions of one of the most extraordinary men of our time. The translation, which is excellent, was revised by Gandhi himself.

SECONDARY READINGS

Birla, G. D. *In the Shadow of the Mahatma: A Personal Memoir*. Bombay, Orient Longmans, 1953.

Private correspondence between Gandhi and his friend Birla, one of India's greatest industrialists, that sheds light on many of Gandhi's activities.

Bondurant, Joan. *The Conquest of Violence*. Princeton University Press, 1958; London, Oxford University Press, 1958; Bombay, Oxford University Press, 1959.

An analysis of Gandhi's political philosophy.

Duncan, Ronald, ed. *Selected Writings of Mahatma Gandhi*. Boston, Beacon Press, 1951; London, Faber, 1951.

A good introductory essay, and a number of interesting selections.

Erikson, Erik H. *Gandhi's Truth: On the Origins of Militant Nonviolence.* New York, Norton, 1969; paperback ed. also.
A psychoanalyst's view.

Fischer, Louis. *The Life of Mahatma Gandhi.* New York, Harper, 1950; London, Cape, 1951; New York, Collier (paperback), 1962.
A detailed sympathetic study.

Gandhi, M. K. *Collected Works.* Vols. 1-42. Delhi, Publications Division of the Ministry of Information and Broadcasting, 1958-71.

—— *Key to Health.* Ahmedabad, Navajivan Publishing House, 1948.
One of the few books, aside from the *Autobiography*, that Gandhi wrote. Gives his views on food, medicine, sex, et cetera.

—— *Constructive Programme: Its Meaning and Place.* Ahmedabad, Navajivan Publishing House, 1941; 2d ed., rev. and enl., 1945.
Outlines his views on economics and education.

—— *Non-Violence in Peace and War.* 2 vols. 2d ed. Ahmedabad, Navajivan Publishing House, 1944.
Collection of Gandhi's speeches and writings.

Nanda, B. R. *Mahatma Gandhi: A Biography.* Boston, Beacon Press, 1958; London, Allen and Unwin, 1958.
Useful narrative account, with good bibliography.

Nehru, Jawaharlal. *Towards Freedom.* New York, John Day, 1941; Boston, Beacon Press, 1958; Toronto, S. J. R. Saunders, 1958. First published under the title *Jawaharlal Nehru: An Autobiography.* London, John Lane, 1936.
Aside from its importance in its own right, this autobiography gives Nehru's interpretation of Gandhi's actions.

Power, Paul F. *Gandhi on World Affairs.* Washington, Public Affairs Press, 1960.

Sharma, J. S. *Mahatma Gandhi: A Descriptive Bibliography.* New Delhi, S. Chand, 1955.
Classified references to the vast literature on Gandhi.

TOPICS FOR DISCUSSION

1. The *Experiments* in comparison with other autobiographies.
2. The significance of the title: Gandhi's attempts to simplify experience.
3. The common background for his various emphases, e.g., vegetarianism, continence, attitude towards Western medicine, economic theories, et cetera.
4. The nature of *ahiṃsa* and *satyāgraha*: the conquest of violence.
5. The importance of fasting: as purification, not as a weapon.
6. What does Gandhi mean when he says "Mind is the root of all sensuality"?
7. The sources of Gandhi's ideas: the transformation of Indian concepts under Western influence.
8. Gandhi's economic ideas as a valid alternative to industrialism.
9. The nature of Gandhi's toleration of other religions and of those who disagreed with him.
10. Gandhi's attitude to caste as exemplifying his attitude towards social reform.
11. The translation of his ideas into a political program; *swarāj* as an expression of truth.
12. Gandhi's autobiography as an illumination of the Indian tradition.

III. Classics of the Chinese Tradition

GENERAL WORKS

CHINESE LITERATURE

Birch, Cyril, ed. *Anthology of Chinese Literature.* New York, Grove Press. Vol. 1 (1965); paperback ed. (Evergreen), 1965; Vol. 2 (1972); paperback ed. 1972.

Representative works of poetry, prose, fiction, and drama from early times to the present century, competently translated by a variety of experts.

Bishop, John L., ed. *Studies in Chinese Literature.* Cambridge, Harvard University Press, 1965.

Chai Ch'u and Winberg Chai. *A Treasury of Chinese Literature.* New York, Appleton-Century, 1965.

An anthology of Chinese prose with generous excerpts from major traditional novels as well as modern fiction.

Chang, H. C. *Chinese Literature: Popular Fiction and Drama.* Edinburgh, Edinburgh University Press, 1973; Chicago, Aldin Publishing Co., 1973.

An anthology of short stories and excerpts from the best-known plays and novels, including *The Water Margin* and *Dream of the Red Chamber.* Each selection is impeccably translated and fully annotated.

Ch'en Shou-yi. *Chinese Literature: A Historical Introduction.* New York, Ronald Press, 1961.

A general survey with much useful information but with serious deficiencies from the scholarly point of view.

Chow Tse-tsung, ed. *Wen-lin: Studies in the Chinese Humanities.* Madison, University of Wisconsin Press, 1968.

Important papers by thirteen scholars, mainly on literature.

Giles, Herbert A. *A History of Chinese Literature.* With a Continuation by Liu Wu-chi. New York, F. Ungar Publishing Co., 1967.

First published in 1901, this pioneer survey is quite out of date, but the continuation by Liu Wu-chi provides a succinct introduction to twentieth-century literature.

Hanan, Patrick. "The Development of Fiction and Drama," in Raymond Dawson, ed., *The Legacy of China.* The Clarendon Press, 1964.

A succinct account, especially good on the beginnings of Chinese fiction and drama.

Hightower, J. R. *Topics in Chinese Literature: Outlines and Bibliographies.* Rev. ed. Cambridge, Harvard University Press, 1962.

A concise and authoritative guide with bibliographical aids.

Hsia, C. T. *The Classic Chinese Novel: A Critical Introduction.* New York, Columbia University Press, 1968; paperback ed., 1972.

An indispensable guide to six major novels, including *The Water Margin, Journey to the West, The Golden Lotus,* and *Dream of the Red Chamber.* With a valuable appendix on the colloquial short story.

Liu Wu-chi. *An Introduction to Chinese Literature.* Bloomington, Indiana University Press, 1966; paperback ed., 1969.

A general survey which, though weak in spots, provides the best introduction to the subject for the beginner. Especially good on the drama. For most purposes, supersedes Ch'en Shou-yi's *Chinese Literature.*

Watson, Burton. *Early Chinese Literature.* New York, Columbia University Press, 1962.

Discusses the literary aspects of Chinese poetry, history, and philosophy in the period ending A.D. 200.

CHINESE THOUGHT

Chan Wing-tsit. *A Source Book in Chinese Philosophy.* Princeton University Press, 1963.

Extensive translations with commentary emphasizing the significance of each new concept to the development of later Chinese thought.

De Bary, Wm. Theodore, *et al. Sources of Chinese Tradition.* New York, Columbia University Press, 1960; paperback ed., 2 vols. 1964.

Source readings in Chinese intellectual history, with introductory essays and commentary.

Creel, Herrlee G. *Chinese Thought from Confucius to Mao Tsê-tung.* University of Chicago Press, 1953; London, Eyre and Spottiswoode, 1954.

A clear, concise account by a scholar especially conversant with classical thought.

Fung Yu-lan. *A History of Chinese Philosophy,* tr. by Derk Bodde. 2 vols. Princeton University Press, 1952-53.

A standard work by a leading contemporary Chinese philosopher. The careful and scholarly translation is a great contribution in itself.

Hughes, Ernest R., ed. and tr. *Chinese Philosophy in Classical Times.* London, Dent, 1942; New York, Dutton, 1942; rev. ed., 1954.

A representative selection of source readings, carefully translated and explained.

Mote, F. W. *Intellectual Foundations of China.* New York, Knopf, 1971.

CHINESE HISTORY

Goodrich, L. Carrington. *A Short History of the Chinese People.* 2d ed., London, Allen and Unwin, 1958; 3d ed., New York, Harper, 1959; reprinted in Torchbook ed.

A concise, factual, and up-to-date survey.

Grousset, René. *The Rise and Splendour of the Chinese Empire,* tr. by Anthony Watson-Gandy and Terence Gordon. London, Geoffrey Books, 1952; Berkeley, University of California Press, 1953; reprinted in paperback ed., 1962.

A general cultural history. No longer wholly up-to-date, but still recommended for its balanced treatment and sensitivity of interpretation.

Latourette, Kenneth Scott. *The Chinese, Their History and Culture.* 2 vols. London and New York, Macmillan, 1934; 3d ed. rev. (2 vols. in 1), New York, Macmillan, 1946. A standard work.

Meskill, John, ed. *Introduction to Chinese Civilization.* New York, Columbia University Press, 1973. An excellent general survey with specialized essays by various scholars.

Reischauer, Edwin O., and John K. Fairbank. *East Asia: The Great Tradition.* Vol. 1 of *A History of East Asian Civilization.* Boston, Houghton Mifflin, 1960; London, Allen and Unwin, 1961. Best available survey of institutional developments.

BIBLIOGRAPHIES

Chan Wing-tsit. *An Outline and an Annotated Bibliography of Chinese Philosophy.* New Haven, Yale University, Far Eastern Publications, 1959; rev. ed., Hanover, New Hampshire, 1953.

Hucker, Charles O. *China: A Critical Bibliography.* Tucson, University of Arizona Press, 1962.

THE ANALECTS (LUN YÜ) OF CONFUCIUS (551–479 B.C.)

The best single source for the ideas of Confucius.

TRANSLATIONS

a. COMPLETE

Legge, James. *The Confucian Analects*, in *The Chinese Classics*, Vol. I. 2d ed. 5 vols. Oxford, Clarendon Press, 1893; reprinted, with minor corrections, notes, and concordance tables, Hong Kong University Press, 1960. Also in *The Four Books*. Shanghai, Chinese Book Company, 1933.

This standard work by a pioneer translator of the Chinese classics into English is still one of the best. Interprets the *Analects* generally as it was understood in later Confucian tradition.

Pound, Ezra. *Confucian Analects*. New York, Kasper and Horton, 1952; London, Peter Owen, 1956.

A poetic interpretation of more value for Pound's unique insights and choice language than for its fidelity to the original text. Recommended only for use alongside other, more scholarly translations.

Soothill, W. E. *The Analects, or the Conversations of Confucius*. London, Oxford University Press, 1937; New York, Oxford University Press, 1941 (Originally published as *The Analects of Confucius*, Yokohama, The Author, 1910).

A dependable translation, with a helpful introduction.

Waley, Arthur. *The Analects of Confucius*. London, Allen and Unwin, 1938; New York, Random House, 1938; reprinted in Modern Library paperback ed.

The translation is recommended for its literary qualities and its attempt to present the work in its historical context rather than in its traditional interpretation. Especially valuable for its introduction explaining the basic terms and concepts appearing in the text.

Ware, James R. *The Sayings of Confucius.* New York, New American Library (Mentor), 1955. (See also *The Best of Confucius.* Garden City, New York, Halcyon House, 1950.) Useful for comparative study with other translations, but highly idiosyncratic.

b. SELECTIONS

Giles, Lionel. *The Sayings of Confucius.* (Wisdom of the East series.) London, John Murray, 1907; New York, Grove Press, 1961.
A substantial selection rearranged under topical headings chosen by the translator.

Hughes, Ernest R., ed. and tr. *Chinese Philosophy in Classical Times.* London, Dent, 1942; New York, Dutton, 1942; rev. ed., 1954. Chapter 2.

Mei, Y. P. Selections in Wm. Theodore de Bary, *et al., Sources of Chinese Tradition.* New York, Columbia University Press, 1960; paperback ed., 2 vols., 1964.

SECONDARY READINGS

Boodberg, Peter A. "The Semasiology of Some Primary Confucian Concepts," *Philosophy East and West*, II, no. 4 (January, 1953), 317-32.

Creel, Herrlee G. *Confucius, the Man and the Myth.* New York, John Day, 1949; London, Routledge and Kegan Paul, 1951. Also under title *Confucius and the Chinese Way.* New York, Harper (Torchbook), 1960.
The most extensive study in English, by a specialist in the field.

Hamburger, Max. "Aristotle and Confucius: A Comparison," *Journal of the History of Ideas*, XX (1959), 236-49.

Kaizuka Shigeki. *Confucius*, tr. from the Japanese by Geoffrey Bownas. London, Allen and Unwin, 1956; New York, Macmillan, 1956.

The life of Confucius against the political and social background of his times, as seen by a Japanese specialist in the period.

Kupperman, Joel. "Confucius and the Nature of Religious Ethics." *Philosophy East and West*, XXI, no. 2 (April, 1971), 189-94.

Liu Wu-chi. *Confucius, His Life and Time*. New York, Philosophical Library, 1955.

A popular introduction.

Sinaiko, Herman L. "The Analects of Confucius," in Wm. Theodore de Bary, ed., *Approaches to the Oriental Classics*. New York, Columbia University Press, 1959; pp. 142-52.

An essay which identifies the values in the *Analects* for humanistic general education. The author is sympathetic to his subject and sophisticated in his evaluation.

Smith, D. H. "The Significance of Confucius for Religion." *History of Religions*, II, no. 2 (Winter, 1963), 242-55.

TOPICS FOR DISCUSSION

1. Confucius' central theme: man in society. His ideal of harmony.
2. The immediate problem: how to govern men and how to govern oneself, Confucius' answer in the noble man or gentleman *(chün tzu)*. The power of political and moral example. The functions of the ruling class.
3. Confucius' humanism in relation to morality and religion. His concept of Heaven. Perfect virtue or humanity *(jen)*, and the principle of reciprocity.
4. Human relations as governed by rites, or decorum, and filial piety.

5. The role of the family in personality development and social relations.
6. The rectification of names; its intellectual and moral significance.
7. Confucius as traditionalist and reformer; as idealist and realist; as "feudal" or "democratic."

THE GREAT LEARNING (TA HSÜEH)

A basic text of the early Confucian school, later canonized in the "Four Books."

TRANSLATIONS

Chan Wing-tsit. *A Source Book of Chinese Philosophy*. Princeton University Press, 1963; pp. 85-94.

Hughes, E. R. *The Great Learning & The Mean-in-Action*. London, Dent, 1942; New York, Dutton, 1943.
A careful translation of the text in its earlier form, with an extensive introduction.

Legge, James. "The Great Learning," in *The Chinese Classics*, Vol. I. 2d ed. 5 vols. Oxford, Clarendon Press, 1893; reprinted with minor corrections, notes and concordance tables, Hong Kong University Press, 1960. Also in *The Four Books*. Shanghai, Chinese Book Company, 1933.
A faithful translation of the "traditional" version as edited by Chu Hsi.

Lin Yutang. "Ethics and Politics," in *The Wisdom of Confucius*. London, H. Hamilton, 1938; New York, Modern Library, 1938.
An accurate and readable translation of the Chu Hsi text.

Pound, Ezra. *Confucius: The Great Digest & Unwobbling Pivot*. New York, New Directions, 1951; London, Owen, 1952.
A stimulating interpretation rather than (strictly speaking) a translation.

SECONDARY READINGS

Fung Yu-lan. *History of Chinese Philosophy*. 2 vols. Princeton

University Press, 1952-53. Vol. I, pp. 361-69.
Hughes, Ernest R., ed. and tr. *Chinese Philosophy in Classical Times.* London, Dent, 1942; New York, Dutton, 1942. Introduction.
Masson-Oursel, P. "La démonstration confucéene—note sur la logique chinoise prébouddhique." *Revue de l'histoire des Religions,* LXVII (1913), 49-54.

Topics for Discussion

1. The *Great Learning* as a guide to self-examination and self-cultivation. The so-called "Eight Steps" *(pa-mu).*
2. The *Great Learning* as a political primer. Its idealism and optimism.
3. Why should the *Great Learning* have merited a place alongside the *Analects* and *Mencius* in the "Four Books" of Confucianism?

THE MEAN (CHUNG YUNG)

A Confucian text of the late Chou period (ca. 4th cent. B.C.), traditionally attributed to Tzu Ssu, Confucius' grandson. Also one of the "Four Books."

Chan Wing-tsit. *A Source Book of Chinese Philosophy.* Princeton University Press, 1963; pp. 97-114.

Hughes, Ernest R. *The Great Learning & The Mean in Action.* London, Dent, 1942; New York, Dutton, 1943.
A careful translation of the older (pre-Chu Hsi) text, emphasizing its metaphysical aspects. There is an extensive introduction.

Ku Hung-ming. "The Central Harmony," in Lin Yutang, *The Wisdom of Confucius.* London, H. Hamilton, 1938; New York, Modern Library, 1938.
A favorite among Chinese readers of English, who consider that Ku captures well the spirit of the text as it has been known to and appreciated by Chinese in the later tradition.

Legge, James. "The Doctrine of the Mean," in *The Chinese Classics*, Vol. I. 2d ed. 5 vols. Oxford, Clarendon Press, 1893; reprinted with minor corrections, notes, and concordance tables, Hong Kong University Press, 1960. Also in *The Four Books.* Shanghai, Chinese Book Company, 1933.
A standard version of the text as edited by Chu Hsi.

See above under *The Great Learning.*

TOPICS FOR DISCUSSION

1. Multiple meanings of the term "Mean." Does it correspond to Aristotle's "Mean"?
2. The ethical and metaphysical significance of "sincerity" (*ch'eng*).
3. The evolution of Confucian thought from the *Analects* to the *Mean*; its relation to Taoism.

MENCIUS (MENG TZU)

The last of the "Four Books," this work expresses the views of Mencius, a leading Confucian thinker (372–289 B.C.).

TRANSLATIONS

a. COMPLETE

Dobson, W. A. C. H. *Mencius.* University of Toronto Press, 1963.
Literary translation by a specialist in ancient Chinese language and literature. Ideal for general education.
Lau, D. C. *Mencius.* Harmondsworth, Penguin, 1970.
A readable and reliable translation.
Legge, James. *The Works of Mencius,* in *The Chinese Classics,* Vol. II. 5 vols. Oxford, Clarendon Press, 1895; reprinted with minor corrections, notes, and concordance tables, Hong Kong University Press, 1960. Also in *The Four Books.* Shanghai, Chinese Book Company, 1933.
Still the standard scholarly translation.
Ware, James R. *The Sayings of Mencius.* New York, New American Library (Mentor), 1960.
A popularized version marred by the translator's proclivity for awkward hyphenated translations of key terms, such as "profit-and-advantage" (for *li*) and "manhood-at-its-best" (for *jen*).

b. SELECTIONS

Giles, .Lionel. *The Book of Mencius.* (Wisdom of the East series.) London, John Murray, 1942.

An extensive selection in a readable translation by a noted Sinologue.

Legge, James. Selections in Lin Yutang, ed. *The Wisdom of China and India.* New York, Random House, 1942; reprinted in Modern Library edition, 1945; pp. 747-84. (This book was also published in England in two volumes as *The Wisdom of China* and *The Wisdom of India.* [London, Michael Joseph, 1944].)

SECONDARY READINGS

Chang, Carsun. "The Significance of Mencius," *Philosophy East and West*, VIII, nos. 1 and 2 (April and July, 1958), 37-48.

Creel, Herrlee G. *Chinese Thought.* University of Chicago Press, 1953; pp. 68-93.

Dubs, Homer H. "Mencius and Sün-dz on Human Nature," *Philosophy East and West*, VI, no. 3 (October, 1956), 213-22.

Fung Yu-lan. *History of Chinese Philosophy.* 2 vols. Princeton University Press, 1952-53. Vol. I, pp. 106-31.

Lau, D. C. "Theories of Human Nature in Mencius and Shyun-tzy," *Bulletin of the School of Oriental and African Studies* (University of London), XV (1953), 541-65.

Liu Wu-chi. *A Short History of Confucian Philosophy.* Harmondsworth, Penguin Books, 1955. Chapters 4, 5.

Munro, Donald. *The Concept of Man in Early China.* Stanford, California, Stanford University Press, 1969. A stimulating and perceptive analysis of early Chinese thought.

Richards, I. A. *Mencius on the Mind: Experiments in Multiple Definition.* London, Routledge and Kegan Paul, 1932; New York, Harcourt, Brace, 1932.

Sargent, G. E. "Le Débat entre Meng-tseu et Siun-tseu sur 'la Nature humaine'," *Oriens Extremus*, III, no. 1 (1956), 1-17.

Shih, Vincent. "Metaphysical Tendencies in Mencius," *Philosophy East and West*, XII, no. 4 (January, 1963), pp. 319-41.

Waley, Arthur. *Three Ways of Thought in Ancient China*. London, Allen and Unwin, 1939, pp. 115-95; New York, Macmillan, 1940; New York, Doubleday (Anchor), 1956, pp. 83-147.

Wu, John C. H. "Mencius' Philosophy of Human Nature and Natural Law," *Chinese Culture*, I, no. 1 (1957), 1-19.

TOPICS FOR DISCUSSION

1. Mencius' juxtaposition of virtue and profit in government. His idealism in an age of power politics and brutality.
2. The kingly way versus the way of the overlord or despot. Ethical cultivation and social action; Mencius' awareness of institutional problems. His Utopian vision.
3. His definition of the problem of human nature; its implications for his political and economic philosophy.
4. Democratic and aristocratic tendencies in Mencius. Significance to him of "the people."
5. Mencius as a defender and definer of Confucianism against the attacks of others.
6. The wide scope of Mencius' thought; his contributions to the development of Confucian thought.
7. The personality of Mencius as it appears in the text.

MO TZU, OR MO TI

An important alternative to Confucianism in the late 5th and early 4th centuries B.C.

TRANSLATIONS

a. COMPLETE

Mei, Y. P. *The Ethical and Political Works of Motse.* London, Probsthain, 1929.
An accurate, readable translation which omits only the chapters of doubtful authenticity or later date.

b. SELECTIONS

Hughes, Ernest R. *Chinese Philosophy in Classical Times.* London, Dent, 1942; New York, Dutton, 1942; rev. ed., 1954, pp. 43-67.
Mei, Y. P. Selections in Wm. Theodore de Bary, *et al., Sources of Chinese Tradition.* New York, Columbia University Press, 1960; paperback ed., 2 vols., 1964.
Watson, Burton. *Basic Writings of Mo Tzu, Hsün Tzu,* and *Han Fei Tzu.* New York, Columbia University Press, 1967.
Contains a translation of selected chapters representing Mo Tzu's essential ideas.
———— *Mo Tzu: Basic Writings.* New York, Columbia University Press, 1963.
Identical to the Mo Tzu section of the above.

SECONDARY READINGS

Chuang Tzu (judgment of Mo Tzu in the T'ien Hsia [World of

Thought] chapter). In Wm. Theodore de Bary, *et. al.* *Sources of Chinese Tradition.* New York, Columbia University Press, 1960, pp. 80-83; paperback ed., 2 vols., 1964, I, 78-81.

Creel, Herrlee G. *Chinese Thought.* University of Chicago Press, 1953; pp. 46-66.

Dobson, W. A. C. H. "Micius," in Douglas Grant, and Millar MacLure, eds., *The Far East: China and Japan.* University of Toronto Press, 1961; pp. 299-310.

Fung Yu-lan. *History of Chinese Philosophy.* 2 vols. Princeton University Press, 1952-53. Vol. I, pp. 76-105.

Hu Shih. *The Development of the Logical Method in Ancient China.* Shanghai, Oriental Book Co., 1922; pp. 63-82.

Maspero, H. "Notes sur la logique de Mo-Tseu et de son école," *T'oung Pao*, XXV (1928), 1-64.

Mei, Y. P. *Motse, the Neglected Rival of Confucius.* London, Probsthain, 1934.

Needham, Joseph. *Science and Civilisation in China.* Cambridge University Press, 1954-   . Vol. II (1956), pp. 165-84.

Waley, Arthur. *Three Ways of Thought in Ancient China.* London, Allen and Unwin, 1939; New York, Macmillan, 1940, pp. 163-81; New York, Doubleday (Anchor), 1956, pp. 121-35.

TOPICS FOR DISCUSSION

1. Mo Tzu's utilitarianism and its social basis.
2. His religious activity and zeal. Does his rigorism or puritanism derive from his religious views, from moral idealism, from a particular view of human nature?
3. Mo Tzu's concept of universal love versus the differentiated love of the Confucianists.
4. Mo Tzu's methods of argumentation and criteria of proof or value.
5. Idealism and totalitarianism in Mo Tzu's political philoso-

phy and in Mo-ism as an organized movement.

6. Mo Tzu as an intellectual and as a reformer. The *Chuang Tzu's* judgment of him as an individual.

7. Mo Tzu and Mao Tse-tung: resemblances and differences.

8. Mo Tzu as an observer and critic of Confucianism.

LAO TZU, OR TAO-TE CHING

The basic text of Taoism which has become a world classic.
Date and authenticity are still much disputed.

TRANSLATIONS

Bynner, Witter. *The Way of Life According to Lao Tzu.* New York, John Day, 1944; London, Editions Poetry, 1946.
More a stimulating poetic interpretation than a translation.
Chan Wing-tsit. *The Way of Lao Tzu.* Indianapolis, Bobbs-Merrill, 1963.
A careful translation based on extensive study of Chinese commentaries.
Ch'u Ta-kao. *Tao Te Ching.* 5th ed. London, Allen and Unwin, 1959; New York, Macmillan, 1959.
A much-used version, based on a rearrangement of the text by the modern Chinese scholar Ch'en Chu.
Duyvendak, J. J. L. *Tao Te Ching: The Book of the Way and Its Virtue.* London, John Murray, 1954.
A competent and at the same time highly original translation by an eminent sinologue. His rearrangement of the text and purely naturalistic interpretation of it, however, have little support either in tradition or among other recent authorities.
Lau, D. C. *Lao Tzu Tao Te Ching.* Baltimore, Penguin Books, 1963.
Lin Yutang. "The Book of Tao," in *The Wisdom of Lao Tse.* New York, Random House (Modern Library), 1948; London, Michael Joseph, 1958. See also *The Wisdom of China and India* (New York, Random House, 1942; for other editions, see above, under *Mencius*).
The first version is a skillful, non-scholarly translation,

interspersed with extracts from the *Chuang Tzu* which serve
as a kind of commentary on the verses of Lao Tzu. This
treatment has the disadvantage, however, of obscuring
somewhat the features of the original work, and giving
instead a composite anthology of early Taoism. From this
standpoint the uninterrupted version in *The Wisdom of
China and India* may be preferable.

Waley, Arthur. *The Way and Its Power: A Study of the Tao Te
Ching and Its Place in Chinese Thought.* London, Allen and
Unwin, 1934; Boston, Houghton, 1935; New York, Grove
(Evergreen), 1958.

An original translation with a lengthy introduction, both
reflecting the astute scholarship and literary finish that are
characteristic of Waley. His rigorous method of reconstruct-
ing the historical and linguistic context as a basis for
interpretation, rather than accepting the traditional or
"scriptural" view, has its own difficulties, however. In this
case there is sometimes a tendency to interpret the *Tao-te
ching* perhaps too narrowly as a dialogue between quietists
and realists (legalists) in the third century B.C.

Wu, John C. H. *Tao Teh Ching.* Jamaica, N. Y., St. John's
University Press, 1961.

A graceful and poetic translation of the text by one for
whom it represents a living tradition, not a philological
exercise.

Secondary Readings

Boodberg, Peter A. "Philological Notes on Chapter One of the
Lao Tzu," *Harvard Journal of Asiatic Studies*, XXX, nos.
3-4 (1957), 598-618.

Chang Chung-yuan. *Creativity and Taoism.* New York, Julian
Press, 1963.

Ch'en, Ellen M. "Is There a Doctrine of Physical Immortality
in the Tao Te Ching?" *History of Religions*, XII, no. 3
(1973), 231-47.

Creel, Herrlee G. *Chinese Thought.* University of Chicago Press, 1953. Chapter VI.

Dubs, Homer H. "The Date and Circumstances of the Philosopher Lao-dz," *Journal of the American Oriental Society,* XLI (1941), 215-21; XLII (1942), 8-13, 300-4; XLIV (1944), 24-27.

Fung Yu-lan. *History of Chinese Philosophy.* 2 vols. Princeton University Press, 1952-53. Vol. I, pp. 170-91.

Hu Shih. "A Criticism of Some Recent Methods Used in Dating Lao Tzu," *Harvard Journal of Asiatic Studies,* II, nos. 3-4 (1937), 373-97.

Kaltenmark, Max. *Lao Tzu and Taoism.* Stanford, California, Stanford University Press, 1969.

Kimura Eiichi. "A New Study on Lao-tzu," *Philosophical Studies of Japan,* I (1959), 85-104.

Maspero, Henri. *Le Taoïsme* (Vol. II of *Mélanges Posthumes sur les Religions et l'Histoire de la Chine*). Paris, Musée Guimet, 1950; pp. 227-42.

Needham, Joseph. *Science and Civilisation in China.* Cambridge University Press, 1954- . Vol. II (1956), pp. 33-127.

Waley, Arthur. *The Way and Its Power* (see above), pp. 17-137.

Welch, Holmes. *The Parting of the Way: Lao Tzu and the Taoist Movement.* Boston, Beacon Press, 1957; London, Methuen, 1958; pp. 18-87.

TOPICS FOR DISCUSSION

1. The multiple meanings of the term "Way" *(Tao):* as a way of life; as the Way of Nature or Cosmic Process; as the One, the First Principle or Absolute; as Nothing.
2. The "natural" and "artificial" in Taoism and Confucianism.
3. Individual life and human values in relation to the Way. Lao Tzu as a critic of civilization, of humanism.

4. *Wu-wei* (non-action, non-striving, effortlessness) as a guide to life; as a way of government.
5. Lao Tzu as social reformer and "anti-hero."
6. Lao Tzu "has insight into what is crooked (bent) but not what is straight" (Hsün Tzu).

CHUANG TZU

A philosophical work of the Taoist school, attributed to Chuang Chou, ca. 369–286 B.C.

TRANSLATIONS

a. COMPLETE

Giles, Herbert A. *Chuang Tzu, Mystic, Moralist and Social Reformer.* 2d ed. London, B. Quaritch, 1926; Shanghai, Kelly and Walsh, 1926; London, Allen and Unwin, 1961.
A free but not inaccurate translation into a Victorian English style, somewhat incongruous with Chuang Tzu.

Legge, James. *The Writings of Kwang-tsze.* (Sacred Books of the East, vol. 40.) Oxford, Clarendon Press, 1891. Also published under title *The Texts of Taoism.* New York, Julian Press, 1959.
A pioneering effort, this rather literal-minded rendering loses much of the wit and fancy of the original.

Watson, Burton. *The Complete Works of Chuang Tzu.* New York, Columbia University Press, 1968.
An excellent translation.

b. SELECTIONS

Fung Yu-lan. *Chuang Tzu: A New Selected Translation with an Exposition of the Philosophy of Kuo Hsiang.* Shanghai, Commercial Press, 1931; repr. New York, Paragon Book Reprint Corp., 1964.
The first seven chapters of the *Chuang Tzu* translated with extensive commentary from the philosopher Kuo Hsiang (3d cent. A.D.) by a leading contemporary Chinese authority.

Out of print and difficult to obtain, but probably the best translation of Chuang Tzu as far as it goes.

Giles, Lionel, ed. *Musings of a Chinese Mystic: Selections from the Philosophy of Chuang Tzu.* (Wisdom of the East series.) London, John Murray, 1906.
Representative selections drawn from the translation of Herbert A. Giles and arranged topically, with a helpful introduction by the editor.

Hughes, Ernest R. *Chinese Philosophy in Classical Times.* London, Dent, 1942; New York, Dutton, 1942; rev. ed., 1954; pp. 165-211.

Lin Yutang, ed. *The Wisdom of China and India.* New York, Random House, 1942; pp. 625-91. (For other editions, see above, under *Mencius.*)
Substantial selections from eleven of the thirty-three chapters of Chuang Tzu.

────── "The Book of Tao," in *The Wisdom of Laotse.* New York, Random House (Modern Library), 1948.

Waley, Arthur. *Three Ways of Thought in Ancient China.* London, Allen and Unwin, 1939, pp. 17-112; New York, Doubleday (Anchor), 1956, pp. 5-79.

Watson, Burton. *Chuang Tzu: Basic Writings.* New York, Columbia University Press, 1964.
A translation designed for the general reader.

SECONDARY READINGS

Creel, Herrlee G. *Chinese Thought.* University of Chicago Press, 1953; pp. 94-114.

────── "The Great Clod: A Taoist Conception of the Universe," in Chow Tse-tsung, ed., *Wen-lin: Studies in the Chinese Humanities.* University of Wisconsin Press, 1968; pp. 257-68.

────── *What is Taoism? And Other Studies in Chinese Cultural History.* Chicago, University of Chicago Press, 1970.

Fung Yu-lan. *History of Chinese Philosophy.* 2 vols. Princeton

University Press, 1952-53. Vol. I, pp. 221-45.

Graham, A. C. "Chuang Tzu's Essay on Seeing Things as Equal," *History of Religions*, IX (nos. 2 and 3, November and February, 1969-70), pp. 137-59.

Hu Shih. *The Development of the Logical Method in Ancient China.* Shanghai, Oriental Book Co., 1922; pp. 140-48.

Wu, John C. H. "The Wisdom of Chuang Tzu: A New Appraisal," *International Philosophical Quarterly*, III, no. 1 (February, 1963), 5-36.

TOPICS FOR DISCUSSION

1. The Way (*Tao*) as conceived by Lao Tzu and Chuang Tzu.
2. Skepticism and mysticism in Chuang Tzu.
3. Chuang Tzu's radical individualism. His conception of the sage.
4. Chuang Tzu and Lao Tzu as social reformers.
5. Romanticism and realism in Chuang Tzu's approach to the conduct of life.
6. Creativity and vitalism as basic themes in Taoism.
7. "Chuang Tzu was prejudiced in favor of nature and did not know man" (Hsün Tzu).

HSÜN TZU, OR HSÜN CH'ING

Writings of a leading thinker and formulator of Confucian teaching in the 3d cent. B.C.

TRANSLATIONS

Dubs, Homer H. *The Works of Hsün Tze.* London, Probsthain, 1928.
A scholarly translation of the greater part of the *Hsün Tzu* text, affording a good over-all view of his philosophy.

Duyvendak, J. J. L. "Hsün-tzu on the Rectification of Names," *T'oung Pao,* XXIII (1924), 221-54. A translation of chapter 22 of the *Hsün Tzu.* Also translated by Y. P. Mei in "Hsun-tzu on Terminology," *Philosophy East and West,* I (1951), 51-66.

Hughes, Ernest R. *Chinese Philosophy in Classical Times.* London, Dent, 1942; New York, Dutton, 1942 (rev. ed., 1954). Chapter 16.

Mei, Y. P. Selections from chapters 17, 19, 22, and 23, in Wm. Theodore de Bary, *et al., Sources of Chinese Tradition.* New York, Columbia University Press, 1960; paperback ed., 2 vols., 1964.

Watson, Burton. *Basic Writings of Mo Tzu, Hsün Tzu, and Han Fei Tzu.* New York, Columbia University Press, 1967.
Contains a major portion of the *Hzün Tzu* translated in an accurate, readable manner for college and general use.

—— *Hsün Tzu: Basic Writings.* New York, Columbia University Press, 1963.
Identical to the Hsün Tzu section of the above.

SECONDARY READINGS

Creel, Herrlee G. *Chinese Thought*. University of Chicago Press, 1953; pp. 115-34.

Dubs, Homer H. *Hsüntze, the Moulder of Ancient Confucianism*. London, Probsthain, 1927; Milwaukee, Caspar, Krueger, Dory, 1930.
The fullest study of Hsün Tzu in a Western language.

Duyvendak, J. J. L. "The Chronology of Hsün-tzu," *T'oung Pao*, XXVI (1929), 73-95.

—— "Notes on Dubs' Translation of Hsün Tzu," *T'oung Pao*, XXIX (1932), 1-42.

Lau, D. C. "Theories of Human Nature in Mencius and Shyun-tzy," *Bulletin of the School of Oriental and African Studies* (University of London), XV (1953), 541-65.

Liu Wu-chi. *A Short History of Confucian Philosophy*. Harmondsworth, Penguin Books, 1955; pp. 90-104.

Shih, Vincent Y. C. "Hsüntzu's Positivism," *Tsing Hua Journal*, IV, no. 2 (February, 1964), 162-73.

TOPICS FOR DISCUSSION

1. Hsün Tzu's defense of scholarship and the intellectual life as opposed to mysticism. His conception of the sage.
2. His view of Heaven and man's relation to it.
3. Hsün Tzu's concept of "human nature" and theory of human nature as evil; the issue between him and Mencius.
4. The importance of discipline in (a) the social order; (b) self-cultivation.
5. Rites or Decorum (*li*); varied functions and profound, even cosmic, significance for Hsün Tzu.
6. Hsün Tzu's political and social philosophy. To what extent is it authoritarian or liberal? To what extent does it derive from his view of human nature?
7. Hsün Tzu and the influence of Taoism in Confucian thought.

HAN FEI TZU

The fullest theoretical statement and synthesis of the ancient Chinese school known as Legalism (Fa chia).

TRANSLATIONS

a. COMPLETE

Liao, W. K. *The Complete Works of Han Fei Tzu.* 2 vols. London, Probsthain, 1939-59.
A complete translation of the text, though the attribution of much of it to the historical figure Han Fei Tzu is doubtful. The rendering is smooth and generally accurate. Note should be taken, however, of the translator's procedure as explained in the methodological introduction to Vol. I.

b. SELECTIONS

Hughes, Ernest R., ed. and tr. *Chinese Philosophy in Classical Times.* London, Dent, 1942; New York, Dutton, 1942; rev. ed., 1954; pp. 254-68.
Mei, Y. P. Selections from chapters 49 and 50, in Wm. Theodore de Bary, *et al. Sources of Chinese Tradition.* New York, Columbia University Press, 1960; paperback ed., 2 vols., 1964.
Watson, Burton. *Basic Writings of Mo Tzu, Hsün Tzu, and Han Fei Tzu.* New York, Columbia University Press, 1967.
Contains an accurate, readable translation of sections 5, 6, 7, 8, 9, 10, 12, 13, 17, 18, 49, and 50.
—— *Han Fei Tzu: Basic Writings.* New York, Columbia University Press, 1964.
Identical to the Han Fei Tzu section of the above.

SECONDARY READINGS

Creel, Herrlee G. *Chinese Thought*. University of Chicago Press, 1953; pp. 135-38.
———— "The Fa-chia: Legalists or Administrators?", *Bulletin of the Institute of History and Philology* (Academia Sinica, Taipei, Taiwan), Extra volume no. IV (1961).
Duyvendak, J. J. L. *The Book of Lord Shang . . . a Classic of the Chinese School of Law*. London, Probsthain, 1928.
For the background of Legalist thought.
Fung Yu-lan. *History of Chinese Philosophy*. 2 vols. Princeton University Press, 1952-53. Vol. I, pp. 312-36.
Hsiao, K. C. "Legalism and Autocracy in Traditional China," *Tsing Hua Journal*, IV, no. 2 (February, 1964), 108-21.
Liang Ch'i-ch'ao. *A History of Chinese Political Thought During the Early Tsin Period*, tr. by L. T. Chen. London, Kegan Paul, 1930; New York, Harcourt, Brace, 1930; pp. 113-38.
Waley, Arthur. *Three Ways of Thought in Ancient China*. London, Allen and Unwin, 1939, pp. 199-255; New York, Doubleday (Anchor), 1956, pp. 151-96.

TOPICS FOR DISCUSSION

1. The essence and scope of law (*fa*) in Han Fei Tzu. Its relation to punishments and the definition of official functions.
2. Government by laws (legalism) versus government by men (Confucianism), as a basic dichotomy of traditional Chinese thought.
3. The evil nature of man as a premise of both Hsün Tzu and Han Fei Tzu.
4. Effortless (*wu-wei*) government as a political ideal in Taoism and Legalism. The science of rulership in Han Fei Tzu.

5. The Legalist view of history and tradition; critique of Confucianism.
6. Does Han Fei Tzu repudiate morality in government?

WORKS OF CHU HSI

Leading exponent and synthesizer of the rationalistic school of Neo-Confucianism in the 12th cent. A.D. *which became orthodox state teaching in later centuries and spread throughout the Far East.*

TRANSLATIONS

a. COMPLETE

Bruce, Joseph Percy. *The Philosophy of Human Nature.* London, Probsthain, 1922.

Translations from the conversations and writings of Chu Hsi as topically arranged in his Collected Works, chaps. 42-48, under classified headings representing the major concepts of his philosophy. The translation, a painstaking and pioneering effort, is generally accurate. The original work, however, was compiled for persons already familiar with the Confucian tradition and the problems of Neo-Confucian philosophy. This makes a direct approach to Chu Hsi through the original source difficult. Bruce meant it to be read together with the companion volume listed below under Secondary Readings.

Chan Wing-tsit. *Reflections on Things at Hand.* New York, Columbia University Press, 1967.

An accurate, complete translation of the *Chin-ssu lu* with an exhaustive scholarly apparatus.

Graf, Olaf. *Djin-Si lu.* 3 vols. Tokyo, Sophia University Press, 1953.

A massive work, providing a German translation of Chu Hsi's classic anthology of four Neo-Confucian masters

(*Chin-ssu lu*). It is extensively annotated and includes a substantial introduction.

b. SELECTIONS

Chan Wing-tsit. Selections, in *A Source Book of Chinese Philosophy*. Princeton University Press, 1963; pp. 593-653.
—— Selections, in Wm. Theodore de Bary, *et al. Sources of Chinese Tradition*. New York, Columbia University Press, 1960; paperback ed., 2 vols., 1964.
Pang Ching-jen. *L'idée de Dieu chez Malebranche et l'idée de li chez Tchou Hi*. Paris, J. Vrin, 1942. Translation of chapter 49 of Chu Hsi's work.
Wieger, Leon, ed. *Textes Philosophiques*. Hsien Hsien, Mission Catholique, 1906; pp. 187-254.

SECONDARY READINGS

Abe Yoshio. "Development of Neo-Confucianism in Japan, Korea, and China: A Comparative Study," *Acta Asiatica*, 17-19 (1969-70), pp. 16-39.
Bernard, Henri. "Chu Hsi's Philosophy and Its Interpretation by Leibniz," *T'ien Hsia Monthly*, V (1937), 9-13.
Bruce, Joseph Percy. *Chu Hsi and His Masters*. London, Probsthain, 1923.
Chang, Carsun. *The Development of Neo-Confucian Thought*. New York, Bookman Associates, 1957; pp. 243-331.
De Bary, Wm. Theodore. "A Reappraisal of Neo-Confucianism," in Arthur F. Wright, ed., *Studies in Chinese Thought* (Comparative Studies of Cultures and Civilizations). University of Chicago Press, 1953; pp. 81-111.
—— "Some Common Tendencies in Neo-Confucianism," in Davis S. Nivison and Arthur F. Wright, eds., *Confucianism in Action* (Stanford Studies in the Civilizations of Eastern Asia). Stanford University Press, 1959; pp. 25-49.
Forke, Alfred. *Geschichte der neueren chinesischen Philoso-*

phie. Hamburg, Friederichsen, de Gruyter, 1938; pp. 164-202.

Fung Yu-lan. *History of Chinese Philosophy.* 2 vols. Princeton University Press, 1952-53. Vol. II, pp. 533-71.

Graf, Olaf. *Djin-Si lu.* 3 vols. Tokyo, Sophia University Press, 1953. Vol. I.

Graham, A. C. *Two Chinese Philosophers: Ch'eng Ming-tao and Ch'eng Yi-ch'uan.* London, Lund Humphries, 1958. An excellent study of two of Chu Hsi's predecessors.

Hocking, W. E. "Chu Hsi's Theory of Knowledge," *Harvard Journal of Asiatic Studies,* I, no. 1 (1936), 109-27.

Hsü, P. C. *Ethical Realism in Neo-Confucian Thought.* New York, 1933; Peiping, 1933; pp. 25-146.

Hughes, Ernest R. *The Great Learning & The Mean-in-Action.* London, Dent, 1942; New York, Dutton, 1943; pp. 167-71.

Le Gall, Stanislas. *Le Philosophe Tchou Hi, sa doctrine, son influence.* Shanghai, Mission Catholique, 1894.

Sargent, Galen E. "Les Débats Personnels de Tchou Hi en Matière de Méthodologie," *Journal Asiatique,* CCXLIII (1955), 213-28.

———— *Tchou Hi contre le Bouddhisme.* Paris, Imprimerie Nationale, 1955.

Shirokauer, Conrad. "Chu Hsi's Political Career: A Study in Ambivalence," in Arthur F. Wright and D. Twitchett, eds., *Confucian Personalities.* Stanford University Press, 1962.

Tomoeda Ryūtarō. "The Characteristics of Chu Hsi's Thought," *Acta Asiatica,* 20-21 (1971), pp. 52-72.

TOPICS FOR DISCUSSION

1. The ideal of Sagehood as compared to the ideal of the Bodhisattva; as a human ideal.
2. The *Reflections on Things at Hand* as a manual of Sagehood and its practice.
3. Neo-Confucianism as the philosophy of human nature.

4. Humanity (*jen*) as both a cosmic and an ethical force.
5. The Neo-Confucian reaffirmation of the goodness of human nature against Buddhist pessimism. Chu Hsi's handling of the problem through such concepts as the original or essential nature and the physical nature; the moral mind and the human mind.
6. Basic concepts in Neo-Confucian metaphysics: the Supreme Ultimate (*t'ai-chi*); Principle (*li*), and ether or material force (*ch'i*). The significance of these in relation to Taoism and Buddhism, Plato, Aristotle, St. Thomas Aquinas.
7. Political implications of Chu Hsi's philosophy.

WORKS OF WANG YANG-MING

Neo-Confucian philosopher of the 15th-16th centuries A.D., *whose philosophy of the Mind provided the principal alternative to Chu Hsi's rationalism in later Chinese thought.*

TRANSLATIONS

a. COMPLETE

Chan Wing-tsit. *Instructions for Practical Living and Other Neo-Confucian Writings by Wang Yang-ming.* New York, Columbia University Press, 1963.
Includes complete translations of "Instructions for Practical Living," "Inquiry on the *Great Learning*," etc., by a leading contemporary scholar of Neo-Confucianism.
Henke, Frederick Goodrich. *The Philosophy of Wang Yang-ming.* Chicago, Open Court, 1916.
A pioneer study of Wang's basic works, now superseded.

b. SELECTIONS

Chan Wing-tsit. Selections, in Wm. Theodore de Bary, *et al. Sources of Chinese Tradition.* New York, Columbia University Press, 1960; paperback ed., 2 vols., 1964.
Ching Chia-yi. *The Philosophical Letters of Wang Yang-ming.* Canberra, Australian National University Press, 1972.
—— "Wang Yang-ming in Translation; Some Selected Letters," in *Chinese Culture*, XI, no. 2 (June, 1970), 62-68.

SECONDARY READINGS

Cady, Lyman V. *Wang Yang-ming's "Intuitive Knowledge."* Peiping, 1936.

Chang, Carsun. *The Development of Neo Confucian Thought.* 2 vols. New York, Bookman Associates, Inc., 1963. Vol. II, pp. 30-97.

———— *Wang Yang-ming: Idealist Philosopher of Sixteenth-Century China.* Jamaica, N. Y., St. John's University Press, 1962.

———— "Wang Yang-ming's Philosophy," *Philosophy East and West,* V, no. 1 (1955), 3-18.

De Bary, Wm. Theodore, ed. *Self and Society in Ming Thought.* New York, Columbia University Press, 1970. See de Bary's essay "Individualism and Humanitarianism in Late Ming Thought" and T'ang Chün-i's "The Development of the Concept of Moral Mind from Wang Yang-ming to Wang Chi."

Forke, Alfred. *Geschichte des neueren chinesischen Philosophie.* Hamburg, 1938; pp. 380-99.

Fung Yu-lan. *History of Chinese Philosophy.* 2 vols. Princeton University Press, 1952-53. Vol. II, pp. 596-620.

———— *A Comparative Study of Life Ideals.* Shanghai, Commercial Press, 1924.

Hsü, P. C. *Ethical Realism in Neo-Confucian Thought.* New York, 1933; Peiping, 1933; pp. 138-46.

Nivison, David S. "The Problem of 'Knowledge' and 'Action' in Chinese Thought Since Wang Yang-ming," in Arthur F. Wright, ed., *Studies in Chinese Thought.* University of Chicago Press, 1953; pp. 112-45.

T'ang Chün-i. "The Development of Ideas of Spiritual Value in Chinese Philosophy," in Charles A. Moore, ed., *The Chinese Mind.* East-West Center Press, 1967; pp. 188-212.

Wang Tch'ang-tche. *La Philosophie morale de Wang Yang-ming.* Shanghai, T'ou-Sè-Wè Press, 1936; Paris, Geuthner, 1936.

TOPICS FOR DISCUSSION

1. Wang Yang-ming and the ideal of Sagehood. Sagehood and human nature; the identity of mind and principle.

2. Innate knowledge (*liang-chih*) and the goodness of human nature.
3. Wang's philosophy and the tension between knowledge and action in Confucian self-cultivation; his doctrine of the unity of knowledge and action.
4. Wang's teaching as quietistic or activisitic. Wang's own life and character as reflected in his teachings.
5. Buddhist (especially Ch'an Buddhist) influences on Wang; his criticisms of Buddhism.
6. Wang Yang-ming as a reformer; as a traditionalist; his social views.
7. Wang's attitude toward learning, scholarship, culture.

TEXTS OF CHINESE BUDDHISM

The important texts of Chinese Buddhism are of two kinds. There are, first, those from India and other Buddhist lands, which were translated into Chinese and widely accepted as basic scriptures or treatises of the religion in China. Second, there are native Chinese writings, frequently commentaries on the original scriptures, which interpreted Buddhist thought in Chinese terms and in some cases became the basis of characteristically Chinese schools. The two together represent a vast body of literature still inadequately represented in translation.

The LOTUS *and* VIMALAKĪRTINIRDĒSA SŪTRAS *are of the former type. Written originally in Sanskrit and expressive of fundamental Mahāyāna ideas, they were translated into Chinese and became especially important in the development of Buddhism in the Far East.* THE AWAKENING OF FAITH IN MAHĀYĀNA, *though attributed to an Indian author, was probably written in China during the sixth century. The* PLATFORM SŪTRA OF THE SIXTH PATRIARCH *is authentically Chinese and one of the earliest products of the Ch'an (Zen) tradition. Though not without their special difficulties, these texts have been found satisfactory for use in general education.*

THE LOTUS SŪTRA
(SADDHARMA PUNDARĪKA SŪTRA,
OR MIAO FA LIEN HUA CHING)

The most representative text of Mahāyāna Buddhism.

TRANSLATIONS

a. FROM THE SANSKRIT

Burnouf, Eugène. *Le Lotus de la Bonne Loi.* Paris, Imprimerie Nationale, 1852. New ed., Paris, Maisonneuve, 1925.

Hurvitz, Leon. *The Lotus Sūtra.* New York, Columbia University Press, forthcoming.

Kern, H. *The Saddhama-pundarīka, or, The Lotus of the True Law.* (Sacred Books of the East, vol. 21.) Oxford, Clarendon Press, 1884. (Reprint, New York, Dover Publications, 1963.)

b. FROM THE CHINESE

Richard, Timothy. *The New Testament of Higher Buddhism.* Edinburgh, Clark, 1910; pp. 127-261.

A partial translation by a Christian missionary, one of the most colorful and influential figures of the late nineteenth and early twentieth centuries, who tended, as the title implies, to interpret Mahāyāna Buddhism too readily in Christian terms.

Soothill, W. E. *The Lotus of the Wonderful Law, or, The Lotus Gospel.* Oxford, Clarendon Press, 1930.

An abridged rendering into translation and paraphrase by a sinologue known for his contributions to the study of

Chinese thought. The most useful version for general
education.

SECONDARY READINGS

Baruch, W. *Beiträge zum Saddharma pundarīka sūtra* (thesis,
Bonn University, 1937). Leiden, Brill, 1938.
Chan Wing-tsit. "The Lotus Sūtra," in Wm. Theodore de
Bary, ed., *Approaches to the Oriental Classics*. New York,
Columbia University Press, 1959; pp. 153-65.
Davidson, J. Leroy. *The Lotus Sūtra in Chinese Art: A Study
in Buddhist Art to the Year 1000*. New Haven, Yale
University Press, 1954.
Hurvitz, Leon. *Chih-i (538-97): An Introduction to the Life and
Ideas of a Chinese Buddhist Monk*. Mélanges chinois et
bouddhiques, 12. Brussells, l'Institut Belge des Hautes
Études Chinoises, 1962.
A thorough study of the use made of the Lotus Sūtra by the
founder of the T'ien-t'ai tradition in China. The Lotus is the
primary scripture of T'ien-t'ai.
Schulemann, G. *Die Botschaft des Buddha vom Lotus des
guten Gesetzes*. Freiburg im Breisgau, Hender, 1937; pp.
61-99.

TOPICS FOR DISCUSSION

1. The *Lotus*: cosmic religious drama or philosophical discourse? The dramatic scope and style of the work:
   supernatural setting expressed in concrete but extrava-
   gant images. Countless Buddha-worlds and endless world-
   ages give new dimensions of space and time to Buddhism.
2. The doctrine that one ultimate vehicle (*yāna*) replaces
   earlier and, necessarily, limited revelations of truth. The
   use of parables (e.g., the Burning House, the Lost Heir) to
   illustrate this new concept.
3. The supreme Buddha as a "god" among many Buddhas

and Bodhisattvas. The Bodhisattvas (especially Avaloki-
teshvara) as saviors and helpers of mankind.
4. The eternality of the Buddha's teaching. The overshadow-
ing of the historical Buddha, Shakyamuni, as teacher by
the eternal Buddha. Buddhist docetism.
5. Buddhism in the *Lotus* as theistic or atheistic.
6. Salvation for all through devotion (to Buddhas and
Bodhisattvas), simple acts of faith, worship of stupas,
copying the text, etc. Buddhahood tends to supersede
nirvāna as the goal of enlightment. Buddhahood as the
realization of the sameness of all phenomena *(dharma)*.
7. Spells, miracles, jeweled stupas, etc., embodied in art as
stimuli to the religious imagination and practice.

THE VIMALAKĪRTINIRDEŚA SŪTRA (WEI-MO-CHIEH SO-SHUO CHING)

An originally Indian scripture which struck a responsive chord in the minds of Chinese Buddhists and which has always been one of the most cherished texts in the Chinese Buddhist tradition. Coming from the mouth of the sagely, humane layman Vimalakīrti, alien notions such as "emptiness," "non-duality," and "inconceivable liberation" seemed more accessible to the Chinese.

TRANSLATIONS

Fischer, Jacob. *Das Sūtra Vimalakīrti*. Tokyo, The Hokuseido Press, 1969.

Idzumi Hokei. "The Vimalakīrti Sūtra," *The Eastern Buddhist*, III, 1924, and IV, 1925-28.

A readable translation.

Lamotte, Etienne. *L'Enseignment de Vimalakīrti*. Bibliotheque du Meséon, 51. Louvain, Publications Universitaries, 1962.

An excellent translation from the Chinese and Tibetan, but more concerned with reconstituting the original Sanskrit than with seeing the text through Chinese eyes.

Luk, Charles (Lu K'uan-yü). The *Vimalakīrti Nirdeśa Sūtra*. Berkeley, Shambala Publications, 1972.

Robinson, Richard H. *The Sūtra of Vimalakīrti's Preaching*. New York, Columbia University Press, forthcoming.

SECONDARY READINGS

Bunker, Emma C. "Early Chinese Representations of Vima-

lakīrti," *Artibus Asiae*, 30, no. 1 (1968), 28-52.
An interesting study of the artistic repercussions of Chinese fascination with Vimalakīrti.
Demiéville, Paul. "Vimalakīrti en Chine," appended to Lamotte translation (q.v.), pp. 438-55.
Mather, Richard B. "Vimalakīrti and Gentry Buddhism," *History of Religions*, VIII, no. 1 (1968), 60-74.
An excellent treatment of the early years of Vimalakīrti's popularity in China.
See also the appropriate chapters in secondary readings listed under *Supplementary Readings on Chinese Buddhism*.

Topics for Discussion

1. The significance of the Buddha's major disciples' declaring themselves unworthy to go and inquire after the health of a layman.
2. Vimalakīrti as a new Buddhist ideal—the product of thriving Indian commercial centers such as Vaiśālī.
3. Word-play as a dramatic technique in the initial exchange between Vimalakīrti and Mañjusrī.
4. The similarity between the various explanations of nonduality and Neo-Taoist "pure conversations."
5. What does Vimalakīrti's "thunderous silence" signify?

THE AWAKENING OF FAITH IN MAHĀYĀNA (TA-CH'ENG CH'I-HSIN LUN)

A brief but seminal treatise of uncertain provenance which came to have profound influence on many of the traditions of East Asian Buddhist thought.

TRANSLATIONS

Hakeda Yoshito. *The Awakening of Faith in Mahāyāna, Attributed to Aśvaghosha.* New York, Columbia University Press, 1967.
The best English translation, with a very useful commentary by the translator based on traditional exegesis.

Richards, Timothy. *The Awakening of Faith.* London, Skilton, 1961; repr. New York, University Books, 1969.
An unsatisfactory translation, distorted by attempts at Christian interpretation.

Suzuki, D. T. *Açvaghosha's Discourse on the Awakening of Faith in the Mahāyāna.* Chicago, Open Court, 1900.

SECONDARY READINGS

Demiéville, Paul. "Sur l'authenticité du *Ta Tch'eng K'i Sin louen*," *Bulletin de la Maison Franco-Japonaise,* 2, no. 2 (1929), 1-78.
A learned treatment of the origins of the text.

Liebenthal, Walter. "New Light on the *Mahāyāna-Śraddhotpāda Śāstra*," *T'oung Pao,* 46, nos. 3-5 (1959), 155-216.

Suzuki, D. T. *Outlines of Mahayana Buddhism.* New York, Schocken, 1963.

A good general treatment of many of the key ideas of the *Awakening of Faith*.

TOPICS FOR DISCUSSION

1. What is the relationship between the One Mind and the two aspects?
2. How is the arising of ignorance explained?
3. Since the *dharmakāya* is one and the same everywhere, what is the need of the five practices (charity, precepts, patience, zeal, and cessation)?
4. The *Awakening of Faith* as a synthesis of the major trends of Mahāyāna thought.
5. The extremely concise, outline style of the text.

PLATFORM SŪTRA OF THE SIXTH PATRIARCH

An original Chinese work and early statement of Ch'an (Zen) thought.

TRANSLATIONS

a. COMPLETE

Chan Wing-tsit. *The Platform Scripture: The Basic Classic of Zen Buddhism.* Jamaica, N. Y., St. John's University Press, 1963.

Luk, Charles (Lu K'uan-yü). "The Altar Sutra of the Sixth Patriarch," in *Ch'an and Zen Teaching*, series three. London, Rider, 1962; pp. 15-102.
An accurate translation of the greatly enlarged Yüan version.

Wong Mou-lam. *The Sutra of Wei Lang.* London, Luzac, 1944; rev. ed., 1953.
An unsatisfactory translation of the Yüan dynasty version.

Yampolsky, Philip. *The Platform Sutra of the Sixth Patriarch.* New York, Columbia University Press, 1967.
A precise and annotated translation of the earliest manuscripts, with a thorough historical and philological introduction.

b. SELECTIONS

Chan Wing-tsit. Selections in Wm. Theodore de Bary, *et al. Sources of Chinese Tradition.* New York, Columbia University Press, 1960; paperback ed., 2 vols., 1964.

SECONDARY READINGS

Broughton, Jeffrey. *Kuei-feng Tsung-mi's Ch'an Preface*. In preparation.
Provides an introduction to both the early schools of Ch'an and the schools of scholastic Buddhism. Tsung-mi was both Ch'anist and Hua-yen scholar.

Chang Chung-yuan. *Original Teachings of Ch'an Buddhism*. New York, Vintage Books, 1971.
An anthology of texts from the Ch'an tradition, though not the "original" teachings.

Demiéville, Paul. *Entretiens de Lin-Tsi*. Documents Spirituels, 6. Paris, Fayard, 1972.
One of the most powerful expressions of the Ch'an colloquial tradition—a fine translation.

——— *Le Concile de Lhasa*. Paris, Imprimerie Nationale, Presses Universitaires, 1952.
An account of the famous debate held in Tibet in the late eighth century in which Chinese Ch'anists advanced the teaching of "sudden awakening" against the "gradual practice" of the Indian teacher Kamalaśīla.

Hu Shih. "Ch'an (Zen) Buddhism in China: Its History and Method," *Philosophy East and West*, III, no. 1 (April, 1953), 3-24. Also in Sidney Ratner, ed., *Vision and Action: Essays in Honor of Horace M. Kallen on His 70th Birthday*. New Brunswick, Rutgers University Press, 1953; pp. 223-50.
The most reliable statement of the early history of Ch'an in China.

Sasaki, Ruth Fuller, *et al*. *The Recorded Sayings of Layman P'ang: A Ninth-Century Zen Classic*. New York, Weatherhill, 1971.

Suzuki, D. T. *The Zen Doctrine of No-mind: The Significance of the Sutra of Hui-neng (Wei-lang)*. London, Rider, 1958.
Highly subjective and unhistorical treatment of Hui-neng's thought and its later development.

TOPICS FOR DISCUSSION

1. The early history of Ch'an in China: historical fact and mythology as seen in the *Platform Sūtra*.
2. Southern and Northern Ch'an. Attitudes towards other forms of Buddhism.
3. Ch'an as representative of a new "Chinese" Buddhism.
4. The concept of no-thought and the identity of *prajñā* and *dhyāna*.
5. The disunity of the work. Evidences of later accretions.

SUPPLEMENTARY READINGS ON CHINESE BUDDHISM

Readers may wish to consult other texts, surveys, and histories of Chinese Buddhism. Among these the following should prove useful.

Chang Ch'eng-chi. *The Buddhist Teaching of Totality: The Philosophy of Hua-yen Buddhism.* University Park, Pennsylvania State University Press, 1971.
The first survey in English of the intricate field of Hua-yen.

Ch'en, Kenneth K. S. *Buddhism in China: A Historical Survey.* Princeton, Princeton University Press, 1963; paperback ed., 1972.
The only survey of the entire history of Chinese Buddhism, including a good bibliography.

―――― *The Chinese Transformation of Buddhism.* Princeton, Princeton University Press, 1973.

De Bary, Wm. Theodore, *et al. The Buddhist Tradition in India, China, and Japan.*
Contains a number of important selections from Chinese Buddhist literature.

Liebenthal, Walter. *Chao Lun: The Treatises of Seng-chao.* 2nd revised ed. Hong Kong, Hong Kong University Press, 1968.
An interpretive translation of a text which is extremely important in the history of Chinese Buddhism.

Robinson, Richard H. *Early Mādhyamika in India and China.* Madison, University of Wisconsin Press, 1967.
A fine study of fifth-century Chinese Buddhism, including the best translation of most of the *Chao-lun.*

―――― *Chinese Buddhist Verse.* The Wisdom of the East

Series. London, John Murray, 1954; repr. New York, Paragon, 1969.

Takakusu Junjiro. *The Essentials of Buddhist Philosophy.* 3rd ed. Honolulu, University of Hawaii Press, 1956.
A useful survey of the development of the scholastic traditions of East Asian Buddhism.

Wright, Arthur F. *Buddhism in Chinese History.* Stanford, Stanford University Press, 1959; paperback ed., 1970.
A brief and judiciously interpretive overview of Chinese Buddhist history.

Zürcher, Eric. *The Buddhist Conquest of China.* 2nd ed., 2 vols. Leiden, E. J. Brill, 1972.
The standard work on the early history of Buddhism in China, including several translations.

THE WATER MARGIN, OR ALL MEN ARE BROTHERS (SHUI HU CHUAN)

A classic of Chinese popular fiction, narrating the adventures of a band of outlaws in the Sung dynasty.

TRANSLATIONS

Birch, Cyril, tr. "The Plot Against the Birthday Convoy (*Shui hu chuan*, XIV-XVI)," in Cyril Birch, ed., *Anthology of Chinese Literature*, Vol. I. Grove Press, 1965; pp. 451-87.
Buck, Pearl S. *All Men are Brothers.* 2 vols. New York, John Day, 1933; New York, Grove Press, 1957; London, Methuen, 1957. 1 vol. ed., New York, Reynal & Hitchcock, 1937, and several other reprint editions.
A complete translation of the 70-chapter version, done in a style that does not suggest the colloquial of the original.
Jackson, J. H. *Water Margin.* 2 vols. Shanghai, Commercial Press, 1937; repr. New York, Paragon, 1968; paperback ed. also.
A somewhat abridged translation in language which misses the spirit of the original.
Kuhn, Franz. *Die Räuber vom Liang Schan Moor.* Leipzig, Insel-Verlag, 1934.
"Free translation and abridgment of the 100-chapter version" (Hightower).
Shapiro, Sidney. "Outlaws of the Marshes (an Excerpt from the Novel)," *Chinese Literature* (December, 1959), pp. 3-61.
A translation of the Lin Ch'ung saga that corresponds to chapters 6-9 of Pearl S. Buck's version. Done in a simple and idiomatic style that is far closer to the original than Mrs. Buck's stilted over-literalness.

SECONDARY READINGS

a. CHINESE FICTION

Bishop, John L. *The Colloquial Short Story in China: A Study of the San-Yen Collections* (Harvard-Yenching Institute Studies, vol. 14.) Cambridge, Harvard University Press, 1956.

―――― "Some Limitations of Chinese Fiction," in John L. Bishop, ed., *Studies in Chinese Literature.* Harvard University Press, 1965; pp. 237-45.

Hanan, Patrick. *The Chinese Short Story: Studies in Dating, Authorship, and Composition.* Cambridge, Harvard University Press, 1973.

An important contribution to scholarship, but too technical for the beginner.

―――― "The Early Chinese Short Story: A Critical Theory in Outline," *Harvard Journal of Asiatic Studies*, 27 (1967), pp. 168-207.

Presents a theory which is of great value for our understanding of the genre as a whole.

Li Tien-yi, ed. *Chinese Fiction: A Bibliography of Books and Articles in Chinese and English.* New Haven, Yale University Press, 1968.

Lu Hsün (Chou Shu-jen). *A Brief History of Chinese Fiction*, tr. by Yang Hsien-yi and Gladys Yang. Peking, Foreign Languages Press, 1959.

A standard reference. Chapter 15 is about *All Men Are Brothers.*

Ou Itaï. *Essai critique et bibliographique sur le roman chinois.* Paris, Véga, 1933.

Based on Lu Hsün's study.

Průšek, Jaroslav. *Chinese History and Literature: Collection of Studies.* Holland, Dordrecht, D. Reidel Publishing Company, 1970.

Contains many valuable studies of traditional fiction. The colloquial short story is examined in depth in relation to the oral storytelling tradition.

Ruhlmann, Robert. "Traditional Heroes in Chinese Popular Fiction," in Arthur F. Wright, ed., *The Confucian Persuasion*. Stanford University Press, 1960; pp. 141-76.

b. THE SHUI HU CHUAN

Alber, Charles. "A Survey of English Language Criticism of the *Shui-hu chuan*," *Tsing Hua Journal of Chinese Studies*, VII, no. 2 (1969), 102-18.

Demiéville, Paul. "Au bord de l'eau," *T'oung Pao*, XLIV (1956), 242-65.

A review of Richard G. Irwin's book, listed below.

Hsia, C. T. *The Classic Chinese Novel: A Critical Introduction*. New York, Columbia University Press, 1968; paperback ed. 1972.

Chapter 3 deals with *The Water Margin*.

Irwin, Richard G. *The Evolution of a Chinese Novel: Shui-hu-chuan*. (Harvard-Yenching Institute Studies, vol. 10.) Cambridge, Harvard University Press, 1953.

―――― "Water Margin Revisited," *T'oung Pao*, XLVIII (1960), 393-415.

Modifies the author's earlier conclusions in regard to the filiation of the *Shui hu chuan* texts.

Li Hsi-fan. "A Great Novel of Peasant Revolt," *Chinese Literature*, December, 1959, pp. 62-71.

An orthodox Communist appraisal.

Liu, James J. Y. *The Chinese Knight-Errant*. London, Routledge & Kegan Paul, 1967; University of Chicago Press, 1967.

Discusses, among other works of fiction and drama glorifying the knight-errant, the *Shui hu chuan* and plays drawing upon the Liangshan legend.

TOPICS FOR DISCUSSION

1. The composition of the book as episodes of adventure. Inventiveness of the storyteller.

2. The historical and literary evolution of the basic story.
3. Characteristics of the novel reflecting its popular origins. Common literary devices.
4. Structure and unity in the novel. Is there any unifying theme or outlook on life? Is there anything characteristically Chinese about the world these figures move in?
5. The *Shui hu chuan* as a panorama of human types. Effectiveness and depth of characterization.
6. What is the significance of the supernatural framework in which the novel is set? The *Shui hu chuan* as a secular novel.
7. The *Shui hu chuan* as social protest or revolutionary literature. What are the basic social or political values embodied here?
8. The code of behavior implicitly followed by the heroes of the Liangshan band. Their attitude toward food, drink, and sex. Instances of savagery and sadism. Punishment of licentious women.
9. Vengeance as a motive. The band's collective adventures: do they indicate lust for aggression or a desire to carry out the will of Heaven? Is the band as corrupt and unjust in its own way as the hated officialdom?

JOURNEY TO THE WEST, OR MONKEY (HSI YU CHI), BY WU CH'ENG-EN

A highly imaginative, fictional version of Hsüan-tsang's epic pilgrimage to India, by the sixteenth-century novelist Wu Ch'eng-en.

TRANSLATIONS

Avenol, Louis. *Si Yeou Ki, ou Le voyage en Occident*, by Wou Tch'eng Ngen. 2 vols. Paris, Editions du Seuil, 1957.
A complete but poor translation.

Hayes, Helen M. *The Buddhist Pilgrim's Progress. From the Shi Yeu Ki: The Records of the Journey to the Western Paradise.* (Wisdom of the East series.) London, John Murray, 1930; New York, Dutton, 1931.
An adaptation.

Hsia, C. T., and Cyril Birch, trs. "The Temptation of Saint Pigsy (*Hsi yu chi*, XXIII)," in Cyril Birch, ed., *Anthology of Chinese Literature*, Vol. 2. Grove Press, 1972; pp. 67-85
An episode of comic allegory. Not available in *Monkey.*

Richard, Timothy. *A Mission to Heaven: A Great Chinese Epic and Allegory.* Shanghai, Christian Literature Society & Depot, 1913; London, Probsthain, 1914.
A translation of chapters 1-7 and a summary of chapters 8-100.

Waley, Arthur. *Monkey.* New York, John Day, 1944; New York, Grove Press (Evergreen), 1958; Harmondsworth, Penguin Books, 1961.
Though much abridged and containing occasional minor errors, a delightful translation.

Yang Hsien-yi and Gladys Yang. "Pilgrimage to the West: Chapter 27," *Chinese Literature*, no. 5 (1966).

An important chapter translated in its entirety. Not available in *Monkey*.

SECONDARY READINGS

Ch'en Shou-yi. *Chinese Literature; A Historical Introduction.* New York, Ronald Press, 1961; pp. 483-87.

Dudbridge, Glen. *The Hsi-yu Chi: A Study of Antecedents to the Sixteenth-Century Novel.* Cambridge, Cambridge University Press, 1970.

Traces the sources and early versions of the novel, with particular reference to the oral tradition.

―――― "The Hundred-Chapter *Hsi-yu Chi* and Its Early Versions," *Asia Major*, XIV, Pt. 2 (1969), pp. 141-91.

Feuerwerker, Yi-tse Mei. "The Chinese Novel," in Wm. Theodore de Bary, ed., *Approaches to the Oriental Classics.* New York, Columbia University Press, 1959; pp. 177-79.

Hsia, C. T. *The Classic Chinese Novel: A Critical Introduction.* New York, Columbia University Press, 1968; paperback ed., 1972.

Chapter 4 deals with *Journey to the West.*

Hsia, C. T. and T. A. Hsia. "New Perspectives on Two Ming Novels: *Hsi Yu Chi* and *Hsi Yu Pu*," in Chow Tse-tsung, ed., *Wen-lin: Studies in the Chinese Humanities.* University of Wisconsin Press, 1968; pp. 229-45.

Liu Ts'un-yan. "The Prototypes of *Monkey (Hsi Yu Chi)*," *T'oung Pao*, LI, no. 1 (1964).

A scholarly article linking Wu Ch'eng-en's novel to its more primitive versions.

―――― "Wu Ch'eng-en: His Life and Career," *T'oung Pao*, LIII (1967).

An impeccably researched biography of the putative author of the *Hsi-yu chi.*

Lu Hsün (Chou Shu-jen). *A Brief History of Chinese Fiction,* tr. by Yang Hsien-yi and Gladys Yang. Peking, Foreign Languages Press, 1959. Chapters 16 and 17.

Ou-I-Tai. "Chinese Mythology," in *Larousse Encyclopedia of Mythology.* New York, Prometheus Press, 1959; London, Batchworth Press, 1959.

Useful information about the Chinese pantheon, which figures importantly in this novel.

Waley, Arthur. *The Real Tripitaka, and Other Pieces.* New York, Macmillan, 1952; London, Allen and Unwin, 1952.

The title essay, a biography of Hsüan-tsang, provides an illuminating historical perspective to his legendary counterpart in the novel.

Yu, Anthony C. "Heroic Verse and Heroic Mission: Dimensions of the Epic in the *Hsi-yu Chi,*" *Journal of Asian Studies,* XXXI, no. 4 (August, 1972), 879-97.

Topics for Discussion

1. The vernacular novel. Its social origins and relation to the classical tradition.
2. The author's role in bridging the great and little traditions. His class affiliation and status as an artist or intellectual.
3. The form of the work. Its episodic character and unifying themes.
4. The legend of Hsüan-tsang. Its historical and popular significance.
5. The *Journey* as allegory, satire, or farce; as a quest for spiritual fulfillment.
6. The major characters as complementary allegorical figures. Do they represent different aspects of human nature or different philosophical positions?
7. Compare Monkey with Abu Zayd in the *Assemblies of al-Ḥarīrī* as heroic or comic figures.
8. Attitudes expressed toward the "Three Religions," their adherents, and their institutions. Religious syncretism in Chinese life and literature.

9. What light does this novel shed on the characterization of the Chinese as "this-worldly"?
10. Satire of social organizations and practices. Is this social protest?
11. The Chinese mode of imagination compared with the Western, as seen in similar fantastic episodes in *The Odyssey, Don Quixote, The Faerie Queene, Paradise Lost,* and *Faust.*
12. The novel seen in the light of anthropology. Cannibalism: Hsüan-tsang coveted as food. The sick or impotent king and the blighted land. Fertility rites. Primitive religious motifs in Chinese folklore: the Indian influence.

THE GOLDEN LOTUS (CHIN P'ING MEI)

The first Chinese novel to depict bourgeois life in naturalistic terms, by an unidentified sixteenth-century author.

TRANSLATIONS

Egerton, Clement. *The Golden Lotus.* 4 vols. London, Routledge, 1939; New York, Paragon Book Gallery, 1962; rev. ed., 1972.
This translation, a labor of love, preserves the prose text in its entirety. Done with the "untiring and generously given help" of C. C. Shu (Lau Shaw). The revised edition is the first complete, unexpurgated edition.
Kuhn, Franz. *Kin Ping Meh, oder, Die Abenteuerliche Geschichte von Hsi Men und seinen sechs Frauen.* Leipzig, Insel-Verlag, 1930; Wiesbaden, Insel-Verlag, 1955.
An admirable abridgment that retains intact the power and the main incidents of the novel.
Miall, Bernard. *Chin P'ing Mei: The Adventurous History of Hsi Men and His Six Wives.* London, John Lane, 1939; New York, Putnam, 1940; reprint (Capricorn Books ed.), 1962.
A translation of the Kuhn version. Recommended for the general reader. Mistranslations, inherited from the German text, are minor and inconsequential.

SECONDARY READINGS

Bishop, John L. "A Colloquial Short Story in the Novel *Chin P'ing Mei*," in John L. Bishop, ed., *Studies in Chinese Literature.* Harvard University Press, 1965; pp. 226-34.
Feuerwerker, Yi-tse Mei. "The Chinese Novel," in Wm.

Theodore de Bary, ed., *Approaches to the Oriental Classics.* New York, Columbia University Press, 1959; pp. 179-81.

Hanan, P. D. "A Landmark of the Chinese Novel," in Douglas Grant and Millar MacLure, eds., *The Far East: China and Japan.* University of Toronto Press, 1961; pp. 325-35.
A perceptive critique of the *Chin P'ing Mei.*
—— "The Text of the Chin P'ing Mei," *Asia Major* (New Series), IX (pt. I, April, 1961), 1-57.
A detailed examination of the extant early editions and of a few spurious chapters in these editions. Of general interest to the student who wants to know something of the intellectual excitement the novel created when its manuscripts were being circulated.
—— "Sources of the Chin P'ing Mei," *Asia Major* (New Series), X (pt. 1, July, 1963), 23-67.
A thorough study of the sources.

Hsia, C. T. *The Classic Chinese Novel: A Critical Introduction.* New York, Columbia University Press, 1968; paperback ed., 1972.
Chapter 5 deals with *Chin P'ing Mei.*

Lu Hsün (Chou Shu-jen). *A Brief History of Chinese Fiction,* tr. by Yang Hsien-yi and Gladys Yang. Peking, Foreign Languages Press, 1959. Chapter 19.

Topics for Discussion

1. The novel's single authorship and its lesser dependence on the repertoire of professional storytellers. Compare the two versions of the story of P'an Chin-lien's seduction as found in this novel and in *All Men Are Brothers.* Would you say that the character of P'an Chin-lien blossoms only after her removal into the Hsi-men household? Evidence that the novelist occasionally encumbers his story with

episodes that are mere redactions of popular tales of his time.

2. The philosophical implications of the novel when seen against the waning influence of the Neo-Confucian orthodoxy among the intellectual elite of its time. *Chin P'ing Mei* as a study of man's uninhibited enjoyment of sensual pleasure and power over fellow men in a hypothetical state of freedom. Kinship of this theme to the Faust and Don Juan themes in Western literature.

3. Life in a polygamous and promiscuous household: the frank acceptance of sexual pleasure as the only reality in life. The abject condition of women in their masochistic submission to Hsi-men's cruel despotism and in their fierce contention for his favors. Their open contempt for men unable to satisfy their sexual demands.

4. Hsi-men's gruesome death. His flagging virility temporarily aided by aphrodisiac pills and eventually drained by P'an Chin-lien's insatiable sexual appetite. In what sense is P'an Chin-lien a far more frightening character than Hsi-men?

5. Cite specific instances in the novel where decent human feelings temporarily triumph over lust and greed. Contrast Li P'ing-erh with P'an Chin-lien. Is Hsi-men's grief over P'ing-erh's death out of character? Moon Lady as an upholder of Confucian duty.

6. Hsi-men's household as a microcosm of political disorder and corruption in the author's time. Hsi-men's backing by powerful ministers at court and his collusion with local officials. Instances of gross injustice perpetrated by officials.

7. The novel as a Buddhist allegory. Moral retribution and reincarnation as the primary facts of human existence. The author's profounder Buddhist vision of the oppressive meanness of all human pursuits and hence the emptiness of the mundane world. The necessity for

redemption: compare the novel in this respect with the
works of Aeschylus, O'Neill, and Faulkner.

DREAM OF THE RED CHAMBER (HUNG LOU MENG), BY TS'AO HSÜEH-CH'IN (TS'AO CHAN)

An eighteenth-century realistic-allegorical novel of the decline of a great family and its young heir's involvement in the world of passion and depravity.

TRANSLATIONS

Birch, Cyril, tr. "How To Be Rid of a Rival (*Hung-lou-meng*, LXIII-LXIX, extracts)," in Cyril Birch, ed., *Anthology of Chinese Literature*, Vol. 2. Grove Press, 1972; pp. 203-58.
The pathetic tale of Yu Erh-chieh translated in its entirety.
Hawkes, David, tr. *The Story of the Stone*. Vol. 1: "The Golden Years." Harmondsworth and Baltimore, Penguin Books,1973.
Volume 1 of a projected 5-volume translation of the 120-chapter novel. Faithful rendition of the first 26 chapters plus a scholarly introduction to the work for the general reader.
McHugh, Florence, and Isabel McHugh. *The Dream of the Red Chamber*, tr. from the German text of Franz Kuhn. New York, Pantheon Books, 1958; London, Routledge and Kegan Paul, 1958.
A fuller and more powerful version than Chi-chen Wang's, though much less accurate.
Wang Chi-chen. *Dream of the Red Chamber*. New York, Twayne, 1958; London, Vision Press, 1959.
An incomplete but most readable translation. The last forty chapters much abridged.

———— *Dream of the Red Chamber.* New York, Doubleday (Anchor), 1958.

An abridgment of the clothbound edition.

Yang Hsien-yi, and Gladys Yang, trs. "Dream of the Red Chamber (An Excerpt from the Novel)," *Chinese Literature*, no. 6-8 (1964).

Translation of Chapters 18-20, 32-34, 74-77.

SECONDARY READINGS

Ch'en Shou-yi. *Chinese Literature: A Historical Introduction.* New York, Ronald Press, 1961; pp. 584-89.

Ho Chi-fang. "On 'The Dream of the Red Chamber'," *Chinese Literature*, no. 1 (1963), pp. 65-86.

A standard Communist interpretation.

Hsia, C. T. *The Classic Chinese Novel: A Critical Introduction.* New York, Columbia University Press, 1968; paperback ed., 1972.

Chapter 7 deals with *Dream of the Red Chamber.*

Knoerle, Jeanne, S. P. *The Dream of the Red Chamber: A Critical Study.* Bloomington, Indiana University Press, 1972.

Lu Hsün (Chou Shu-jen). *A Brief History of Chinese Fiction,* tr. by Yang Hsien-yi and Gladys Yang. Peking, Foreign Languages Press, 1959. Chapter 24, pp. 298-316.

Spence, Jonathan D. *Ts'ao Yin and the K'ang-hsi Emperor, Bondservant and Master.* New Haven, Yale University Press, 1966.

This historical study casts valuable biographical light on the author of *Dream of the Red Chamber.*

West, Anthony. "Through a Glass, Darkly," *The New Yorker,* November 22, 1958; pp. 223-32.

A review of the Wang and Kuhn-McHugh versions, refreshingly astute and original in its comments on the novel's greatness. An excellent guide for a beginning student.

Westbrook, Francis A. "On Dreams, Saints, and Fallen

Angels: Reality and Illusion in *Dream of the Red Chamber* and *The Idiot*," *Literature East and West*, X, no. 3, pp. 371-91.

A valuable comparative study of two world masterpieces.

Wu Shih-ch'ang. "History of 'The Red Chamber Dream'," *Chinese Literature*, no. 1 (1963), pp. 87-100.

——— *On the Red Chamber Dream: A Critical Study of Two Annotated Manuscripts of the XVIIIth Century.* Oxford, Clarendon Press, 1961.

The interested student may want to read chapter 20, "Summaries and Conclusions," to get a notion of the complex problems attending the novel's authorship and texts.

TOPICS FOR DISCUSSION

1. The novel as autobiography. Compared with *Chin P'ing Mei, Journey to the West,* and *The Water Margin,* why is *Dream of the Red Chamber* a far subtler and more complex novelistic structure in spite of its apparent adherence to the episodic method? Is the autobiographical experience completely objectified as fiction?

2. The novel as tragedy. What constitutes the major tragic conflict in the novel? Is the hero's final action—forsaking the world—understandable? How to reconcile the immense amount of suffering depicted in the novel and the hero's determined quest for personal liberation?

3. The novel of manners vs. allegory. Are the allegorical portions as successful as the realistic portions? Is there a basic ambiguity in the author's attitude toward sexual love? The novel was originally titled *Shih t'ou chi* or *The Story of the Stone.* Discuss the Stone motif.

4. The novel is especially admired in China for its gallery of heroines. Which of the heroines strikes you as the most memorable? How would you characterize Black Jade? Compare the novel with *The Tale of Genji* as to insight into feminine psychology.

5. Many Chinese scholars maintain that the last forty chapters of *Dream of the Red Chamber*, a 120-chapter novel, were "completed" by one Kao Ê, a total stranger to the author. Do you get the impression that the last third of the novel (chapters 39-50 in the Kuhn-McHugh version) is in any way inferior to the first two thirds?

CHINESE POETRY

TRANSLATIONS

Ayling, Alan and Duncan R. Mackintosh. *A Collection of Chinese Lyrics*. London, Routledge and Kegan Paul, 1965; repr. Nashville, Vanderbilt University Press, 1967.
  Pleasing translations of *tz'u* poetry done in rhyme and with accompanying Chinese texts.
Bynner, Witter. *The Jade Mountain*, tr. from the texts of Kiang Kang-hu. New York, Knopf, 1929; London, Allen and Unwin, 1929.
  Translation of a popular anthology. *Three Hundred Poems of the T'ang Dynasty.*
Davis, A. R., ed. *The Penguin Book of Chinese Verse*, tr. by Robert Kotewall and Norman L. Smith. Harmondsworth and Baltimore, Penguin Books, 1962.
  This anthology includes over 120 poets, most of them represented by one short lyric.
Frodsham, J. D. *An Anthology of Chinese Verse: Han, Wei, Chin and the Northern and Southern Dynasties.* Oxford, the Clarendon Press, 1967.
  An ample selection of pre-T'ang poetry, faithfully rendered.
Graham, A. C. *Poems of the Late T'ang.* Baltimore, Penguin Books, 1965.
  Selections from one of the most interesting periods of Chinese poetry; excellent translations and introductory material.
Liu, James J. Y. *Major Lyricists of the Northern Sung.* Princeton University Press, 1974.
  A guide to six *tz'u* poets of the Northern Sung dynasty, with translation and critical analysis of their representative poems.

Payne, Robert. *The White Pony.* New York, John Day, 1947; New York, New American Library (Mentor), 1960.
Though the translations leave much to be desired, this is the most comprehensive anthology for the beginning student.

Waley, Arthur. *Chinese Poems.* London, Allen and Unwin, 1946. Includes selections from *170 Chinese Poems, More Translations from the Chinese, The Temple,* and *The Book of Songs.*
An ample representation of Waley's skill as a translator of Chinese verse, though, in Waley's own words, "not a balanced anthology of Chinese poetry." Half of the book is devoted to Po Chü-i.

Watson, Burton. *Chinese Lyricism: Shih Poetry from the Second to the Twelfth Century.* New York, Columbia University Press, 1971; paperback ed., 1971.
An excellent introduction to *shih* poetry from the Han to the Sung dynasty. Able translation of some 200 representative poems accompanied by illuminating comments.

——*Chinese Rhyme-Prose: Poems in the Fu Form From the Han and Six Dynasties Periods.* New York, Columbia University Press, 1971.
Brilliant translations of thirteen works of the genre.

Both Payne and Waley give generous selections from the SHIH CHING (BOOK OF SONGS). *The interested student should read Waley,* THE BOOK OF SONGS (1937; *New York, Grove Press* [*Evergreen*], 1960), *and Ezra Pound,* THE CONFUCIAN ODES: THE CLASSIC ANTHOLOGY DEFINED BY CONFUCIUS (*Cambridge, Harvard University Press,* 1954; *New York, New Directions,* 1959). *Some major Chinese poets recommended for further reading:*

Ch'ü Yüan. *Ch'u Tz'u: The Songs of the South: An Ancient Chinese Anthology,* tr. by David Hawkes. Oxford, Clarendon Press, 1959; Boston, Beacon Press (paperback ed.), 1962.

Hsin Ch'i-chi. *Hsin Ch'i-chi,* tr. by Irving Yucheng Lo. New York, Twayne Publishers, 1971.

Li Ho. *The Poems of Li Ho (791–817)*, tr. by J. D. Frodsham. Oxford, the Clarendon Press, 1970.

Li Po. *The Poetry and Career of Li Po*, by Arthur Waley. London, Allen and Unwin, 1950; New York, Macmillan, 1950.

Li Shang-yin. *The Poetry of Li Shang-yin, Ninth-Century Baroque Chinese Poet*, by James J. Y. Liu. Chicago, University of Chicago Press, 1969.

Po Chü-i. *The Life and Times of Po Chü-i*, by Arthur Waley. London, Allen and Unwin, 1949; New York, Macmillan, 1950.

Su Tung-p'o. *Su Tung-p'o: Selections from a Sung Dynasty Poet*, tr. by Burton Watson. New York, Columbia University Press, 1965.

T'ao Ch'ien. *The Poetry of T'ao Ch'ien*, tr. by James Robert Hightower. Oxford, the Clarendon Press, 1970.

Tu Fu. *Tu Fu, China's Greatest Poet*, by William Hung. 2 vols. Cambridge, Harvard University Press, 1952; London, Oxford University Press, 1952.

SECONDARY READINGS

Ch'en Shou-yi. *Chinese Literature: A Historical Introduction.* New York, Ronald Press, 1961. Chapter 2, "The Book of Songs," and chapter 12, "The Songs of the T'ang Dynasty."

Chow Tse-tsung, ed. *Wen-lin: Studies in the Chinese Humanities.* Madison, University of Wisconsin Press, 1968.
Seven of the twelve essays included are on poetry.

Hightower, J. R. *Topics in Chinese Literature.* Rev. ed. Cambridge, Harvard University Press, 1962. Chapters 4, 7-10, 14.

Kao Yu-kung, and Tsu-lin Mei. "Syntax, Diction, and Imagery in T'ang Poetry," *Harvard Journal of Asiatic Studies*, Vol. 31 (1971), pp. 51-136.
A major contribution to our understanding of Recent Style poetry (*lü-shih*).

Liu, James J. Y. *The Art of Chinese Poetry.* University of Chicago Press, 1962; London, Routledge and Kegan Paul, 1962.

An excellent guide to the forms, themes, and techniques of Chinese poetry. Ample reference to Western poetry and criticism.

MacLeish, Archibald. *Poetry and Experience.* Cambridge, Houghton Mifflin, 1961; London, Bodley Head Press, 1961.

The author, a distinguished poet, defines the poetic experience with the help of a Chinese classic in poetics, Lu Chi's *Wen Fu.* Read the first four chapters. Chapter 3 discusses the imagery of several Chinese poems.

Waley, Arthur. *170 Chinese Poems.* London, Constable, 1918; New York, Knopf, 1919; new ed. London, Constable, 1962.

Has a good introduction on the themes and techniques of Chinese poetry.

———— *The Temple and Other Poems.* London, Allen and Unwin, 1923; New York, Knopf, 1923.

The introductory section gives a historical survey of *fu* poetry.

Watson, Burton. *Early Chinese Literature.* New York, Columbia University Press, 1962.

The section on Poetry discusses the *Book of Songs,* the *Songs of the South,* and *fu* poetry of the Han period. Dazzling translations of several *fu* poems.

Yoshikawa Kojiro. *An Introduction to Sung Poetry,* tr. by Burton Watson. Cambridge, Harvard University Press, 1967.

A survey of the subject by a great Japanese sinologist.

TOPICS FOR DISCUSSION

1. The Chinese language: its monosyllabic character, its concreteness, its elliptical economy. How do these qualities contribute to the pregnant density of Chinese verse?

2. The use of complementary or contrasting images in a given poem to enhance meaning. Is Western-style metaphor a regular feature of Chinese poetry? Among the poets you have read, is there a conscious use of symbolism?

3. The brevity of Chinese poems. Does the Chinese poet suffer in comparison with the Western poet because he is denied a wider choice of lyrical forms that offer larger scope? Do a close analysis of a Chinese poem, and then examine it again in the larger context of the poet's other works. Does the poem gain in meaning and consequence when seen as part of a larger whole?

4. The themes of Chinese poetry. Compare the love lyrics in *The Book of Songs* with later love poetry. Nature and friendship as themes. Does their habitual fondness for conventional themes and sentiments prevent Chinese poets from reaching the kind of soul-searching honesty that distinguishes the best Western lyrical poetry?

5. The Chinese poet as philosopher. The momentary illumination of Confucian, Taoist, or Buddhist wisdom in the personal context of lyrical emotion.

6. The poet and his masks. Does the Chinese poet always speak in his own voice? The ballad tradition as established in *The Book of Songs*. How good is Chinese narrative poetry?

7. Chinese poetry and the musical tradition. The song quality of Chinese verse compared with the conversational style and colloquial rhythms of much English lyrical poetry.

IV. Classics of the Japanese Tradition

GENERAL WORKS

JAPANESE LITERATURE

Aston, W. G. *A History of Japanese Literature*. New York, Appleton Century, 1899; repr. New York, Johnson Reprint Corp., 1966.

Badly outdated, but still the only history in English.

Bownas, Geoffrey and Anthony Thwaite. *The Penguin Book of Japanese Verse*. Baltimore, Penguin Books, 1964.

Selections from all periods in readable translations.

Brower, Robert H. and Earl Miner. *Japanese Court Poetry*. Stanford, Stanford University Press, 1961.

An excellent study of the development and aesthetics of Japanese poetry from the earliest times until the 14th century, illustrated with many translations.

Keene, Donald. *Japanese Literature: An Introduction for Western Readers*. London, John Murray, 1953; New York, Grove Press (Evergreen), 1955.

An introduction to the major forms of Japanese literature, for the general reader.

―――― *Anthology of Japanese Literature from the Earliest Era to the Mid-nineteenth Century*. New York, Grove Press (clothbound and paperback eds.), 1955.

―――― *Modern Japanese Literature, an Anthology*. New York, Grove Press (clothbound and paperback eds.), 1956.

These two anthologies provide a general survey of Japanese literature, including many of the works listed in this Guide.

Miller, Roy Andrew. *The Japanese Language*. Chicago, University of Chicago Press, 1967.

Important not only for linguists but for students of literature who wish to learn how the Japanese language itself molded the literature.

Miner, Earl. *An Introduction to Japanese Court Poetry*.

Stanford, Stanford University Press, 1968; paperback ed. also.

A simplified version of *Japanese Court Poetry* (see above). It also includes a discussion of 15th century poetry, not covered in the earlier book.

Ueda Makoto. *Literary and Art Theories in Japan.* Cleveland, The Press of Case Western Reserve University, 1967.

An examination of different aspects of Japanese aesthetics as revealed in poetry, drama, landscape gardening, *etc.*

JAPANESE THOUGHT

Anesaki Masaharu. *History of Japanese Religion.* London, Kegan Paul, Trench, Trubner, 1930.

A standard work by an outstanding Japanese scholar of religion.

Tsunoda Ryusaku, Wm. Theodore de Bary, and Donald Keene, eds. *Sources of Japanese Tradition.* New York, Columbia University Press, 1958; paperback ed., 2 vols., 1964.

A source book covering the major developments in Japanese religion and thought from earliest times to the present, with extensive historical introductions to the translations.

JAPANESE HISTORY

Reischauer, Edwin O. *Japan, Past and Present.* 1st ed., London, Duckworth, 1947; 2d ed. New York, Knopf, 1953.

A brief, general survey by a leading authority.

Sansom, Sir George B. *Japan, A Short Cultural History.* London, Cresset Press, 1931; New York, Century, 1931; rev. ed., New York, Appleton-Century, 1943; London, Cresset Press, 1946.

A standard work on Japanese cultural history from antiquity up to modern times. Excellent background reading for the works listed in this guide.

———— *A History of Japan to 1334.* Stanford University Press, 1958; London, Cresset Press, 1959.

———— *A History of Japan 1334-1615.* Stanford University Press, 1961.

———— *A History of Japan 1615-1867.* Stanford University Press, 1963.

These three volumes provide a much fuller account of the political, economic, and social development of Japan. The definitive work of its type.

TEXTS OF JAPANESE BUDDHISM

The Japanese first received advanced continental civilization through Korean Buddhist monks who knew written Chinese. Since all Japanese knowledge of Buddhism was derived from Chinese sources, China became for Japan the "Land of the Buddha." All of the principal sects of Chinese Buddhism were transplanted in Japan; the scriptures were read in Chinese and the commentarial literature was generally composed in that language. Eventually, certain Japanese monks did choose to compose important works in the native language. Of the following selections, Kūkai wrote in an extremely ornate style of literary Chinese, while Hakuin's Zen letters in Japanese represent a style reminiscent of that of the great Sung Ch'an Master Ta-hui Tsung-kao.

WRITINGS OF KŪKAI (KŌBŌ DAISHI)

Kūkai, greatest of the Heian period Buddhist teachers, studied esoteric Buddhism and Sanskrit in the T'ang capital Ch'ang-an and brought back to Japan a type of Buddhism which was to have an enormous impact on Heian culture.

TRANSLATIONS

De Bary, Wm. Theodore, *et al. The Buddhist Tradition in India, China, and Japan.* New York, The Modern Library, 1969.
Contains a section on Kūkai.
Hakeda, Yoshito S. *Kūkai: Major Works.* New York, Columbia University Press, 1972.
Includes a biography of Kūkai, a study of his thought, and translations of his most important works.

SECONDARY READINGS

Bharati, Agehananda. *The Tantric Tradition.* London, Rider, 1965.
A useful discussion of Hindu and Buddhist tantric teachings by a European adherent.
Dasgupta, S. B. *An Introduction to Tantric Buddhism.* Calcutta, University of Calcutta Press, 1950.
Govinda, Lama Anagarika. *Foundations of Tibetan Mysticism.* New York, Samuel Weiser, 1973.
A discussion of Tibetan esoteric teachings.

Tucci, Giuseppe. *The Theory and Practice of the Mandala.* London, Rider, 1961.
   A general discussion of mandala symbolism by a scholar of Indian and Tibetan Buddhism.
Warder, A. K. *Indian Buddhism.* Delhi, Motilal Banarsidass, 1970.
   Contains a section on the great Buddhist universities and *mantrayāna.* Discusses the Kriyā, Caryā, Yoga, and Anuttarayoga systems.
Wayman, Alex. *The Buddhist Tantras.* New York, Samuel Weiser, 1973.
   Read the first section, "Introductions."

TOPICS FOR DISCUSSION

1. The aesthetic element in Kūkai's teaching.
2. Kūkai's attitude toward Confucianism, Taoism, and the esoteric Buddhist teachings.
3. How did Kūkai view the historical Buddha?
4. Usually, the ten stages to enlightenment were thought to take three kalpas (eons). In what way is Kūkai's esoteric Buddhism a "sudden" approach?
5. The literary form of the *Indications of the Goals of the Three Teachings.*

WRITINGS OF THE ZEN MASTER HAKUIN

Hakuin, greatest of the Tokugawa period Zen Masters, restored Rinzai Zen to the purity of its T'ang and Sung traditions.

TRANSLATIONS

De Bary, Wm. Theodore, *et al. The Buddhist Tradition in India, China, and Japan.* The Modern Library, 1969. Contains excerpts from Hakuin's *Orategama.*

Yampolsky, Philip B. *The Zen Master Hakuin: Selected Writings.* New York, Columbia University Press, 1971. Contains a translation of the *Orategama* in its entirety along with two of Hakuin's other writings. The introduction provides a succinct historical survey of the various Zen transmissions to Japan.

SECONDARY READINGS

Dumoulin, Heinrich. *A History of Zen Buddhism.* New York, McGraw-Hill Book Company, 1965. Contains a useful chapter on Hakuin.

Miura Isshū, and Ruth Fuller Sasaki. *Zen Dust.* New York, Harcourt, Brace & World, Inc., 1968. This is an expanded version of *The Zen Kōan* which contains a wealth of information on Zen and Chinese Buddhism in general.

————— *The Zen Kōan.* New York, Harcourt, Brace & World, Inc., 1965. Deals with the history of the *kōan* in Rinzai Zen and *kōan*

study as it is now carried on in Japan.
Shibata Masumi. *Les Maitres du Zen au Japan.* Paris, Maisonneuve & Larose, 1969. In addition to Hakuin, deals with Yōsai, Dōgen, Musō, Ikkyū, Takuan, Suzuki Shōsan, and Bankei.

TOPICS FOR DISCUSSION

1. Meditation in the midst of activity and meditation in quietude.
2. The two levels of truth (the absolute truth and the worldly truth) in Hakuin's sermons.
3. Alchemy and Taoism in Hakuin's letters.
4. *Kōan* study versus "dead sitting."
5. Similarities between meditation on "Mu" and the mindfulness meditation of the *Mahāsatipaṭṭhana sutta* (see Indian section); Hakuin's praise of Hīnayāna adepts.

SUPPLEMENTARY READINGS ON JAPANESE BUDDHISM

Readers may wish to consult other texts, surveys, and histories of Japanese Buddhism. Among these the following should prove useful.

Anesaki Masaharu. *Nichiren, the Buddhist Prophet.* Cambridge, Harvard University Press, 1916.

A study of one of the most fascinating personalities in Japanese history.

Bloom, Alfred. *Shinran's Gospel of Pure Grace.* Tucson, The University of Arizona Press, 1965.

Provides a discussion of the background of Pure-land thought in addition to a detailed study of Shinran's religious development.

Buck, Harry M. "The *Lotus Scripture* in the Nichiren Tradition," in Bardwell L. Smith, ed., *Asian Religions: 1971.* American Academy of Religion, 1971; pp. 17-34.

A useful treatment of the rather special use of the *Lotus* in this remarkable tradition of medieval Japanese Buddhism.

Chan Wing-tsit, *et al. The Great Asian Religions.* London, Collier-Macmillan Limited, 1969.

Contains source readings on early and medieval Japanese Buddhism.

De Bary, Wm. Theodore, *et al. The Buddhist Tradition in India, China, and Japan.* New York, The Modern Library, 1969.

Contains a number of important selections from Japanese Buddhist literature.

Earhart, H. Byron. *Japanese Religion: Unity and Diversity.*

Belmont, California, Dickenson Publishing Company, Inc., 1969.
Places Buddhism in the context of all Japanese religion.
Eliot, Sir Charles. *Japanese Buddhism*. London, Routledge & Kegan Paul, 1959.
A somewhat outdated study, covering India and China as well as Japan.
Fujiwara Ryōsetsu. *The Tanni Shō*. Kyoto, Ryukoku Translation Center (Ryukoku University), 1962.
The *Tanni Shō* is one of the most beautiful expressions of Amidist devotional literature. Other works of Shinran (including his *Kyō Gyō Shin Shō, Jōdo Wasan*, and *Shōshin Ge*) have been published in this series.
Kamstra, J. H. *Encounter or Syncretism*. Leiden, E. J. Brill, 1967.
A detailed study of the initial period of Buddhism in Japan. Though Kamstra's arguments are not universally accepted, they are interesting and useful.
Kitagawa, Joseph M. *Religion in Japanese History*. New York, Columbia University Press, 1966.
A series of lectures on the main themes of Japanese religious history, from the earliest times through the postwar period.
Masunaga Reiho. *A Primer of Sōtō Zen*. Honolulu, East-West Center Press, 1971.
A readable translation of the *Shobōgenzō zuimonki*.
Reischauer, Edwin O. *Ennin's Travels in T'ang China*. New York, The Ronald Press Company, 1955.
A fascinating mosaic of ninth-century China drawn from the diary of an itinerant Japanese monk. Provides insight into Japanese attitudes toward China as the homeland of Buddhism. Companion volume to Reischauer's translation of *Ennin's Diary*.
Takakusu Junjiro. *The Essentials of Buddhist Philosophy*. 3rd ed. Honolulu, University of Hawaii Press, 1956.
A survey of East Asian scholastic Buddhism from a Japanese perspective.

MANYŌSHŪ

A collection of 4,516 poems in various forms, compiled about
A.D. *770 by Otomo Yakamochi and others.*

TRANSLATIONS

Nippon Gakujutsu Shinkōkai. *The Manyōshū.* Tokyo, Iwana-
mi Shoten, 1940; repr. New York, Columbia University
Press, 1965; paperback ed., 1970.
One thousand poems (about a quarter of the entire work)
well translated into English verse with an extensive, if rather
outdated, introduction.
The Manyôśû. 20 vols. plus index. Leiden, E. J. Brill, 1929-64.
A complete translation. Scholarly accuracy rather than
poetic beauty has been the standard.
Vergez, Robert. *Anthologie du Manyōsyū.* Tokyo, Maison
Franco-japonaise, 1949.
Accurate and often poetic translations with an interesting
introduction.
Yasuda, Kenneth. *Land of the Reed Plains: Ancient Japanese
Lyrics from the Manyoshu.* Rutland, Vt., Tuttle, 1960;
Tokyo, Tuttle, 1961.
Selections with illustrations.

SECONDARY READINGS

Brower, Robert H. and Earl Miner. *Japanese Court Poetry.*
Stanford, Stanford University Press, 1961.
Chapter IV, "The Early Literary Period," includes excellent translations of *Manyōshū* poetry as well as a penetrating
discussion of the anthology.

Philippi, Donald L. *Kojiki.* Princeton, Princeton University Press, 1969.
The *Kojiki*, the first Japanese "history," gives the traditional Shinto account of the Age of the Gods and of the foundation of the country. Although the literary interest is slight, the numerous poems provide an illuminating contrast with the *Manyōshū* poetry.
———— *This Wine of Peace, This Wine of Laughter.* New York, Grossman, 1968.
Translations of pre-*Manyōshū* poetry.
Sansom, Sir George B. *A History of Japan to 1334.* Stanford University Press, 1958; London, Cresset Press, 1959.
Chapter 5 describes the historical background of the *Manyōshū*.

TOPICS FOR DISCUSSION

1. The Japaneseness of the *Manyōshū*. Choice of imagery and subject matter. The contrast with Chinese poetry.
2. The *Manyōshū* as the expression of an emerging civilization. Functions of poetry at the time. The court poets. The poets away from the court. Patriotic attitudes.
3. Contrasts in style, subject matter, and form between the *Manyōshū* and later collections of Japanese poetry. Typical features of *Manyōshū* poetry.
4. Individual poets and their characteristic manners: Hitomaro, Akahito, Yakamochi, Okura. Emperors as poets. Women poets.

THE PILLOW-BOOK OF SEI SHŌNAGON (MAKURA NO SŌ-SHI)

A collection of notes and essays, mainly concerned with court life in the late tenth century, by one of Japan's greatest stylists.

TRANSLATIONS

a. COMPLETE

Beaujard, André. *Les notes de chevet de Séi Shōnagon', dame d'honneur au palais de Kyoto.* Paris, Maisonneuve, 1934.
The first complete translation, but almost devoid of literary merit.
Morris, Ivan. *The Pillow Book of Sei Shōnagon.* 2 vols. New York, Columbia University Press, 1967; paperback ed., 1970.
A complete translation of great literary distinction. The second volume is devoted to notes on the text and to many important items of background information.

b. SELECTIONS

Kobayashi Nobuko. *The Sketch-book of the Lady Sei Shōnagon.* London, John Murray, 1930; New York, Dutton, 1930.
A somewhat more generous selection than Arthur Waley's, but an uninspired translation.
Waley, Arthur. *The Pillow-Book of Sei Shonagōn.* London, Allen and Unwin, 1928; Boston and New York, Houghton

Mifflin, 1929; New York, Grove Press, 1953 (Evergreen ed., 1960).
About a quarter of the original work, beautifully translated.

SECONDARY READINGS

Beaujard, André. *Séi Shônagon', son temps et son oeuvre.* Paris, Maisonneuve, 1934.
Sansom, Sir George B. *A History of Japan to 1334.* Stanford University Press, 1958; London, Cresset Press, 1959.
Chapter 9 is especially helpful.
Tsunoda Ryusaku, Wm. Theodore de Bary, and Donald Keene, eds. *Sources of Japanese Tradition.* New York, Columbia University Press, 1958; paperback ed., 2 vols., 1964.
Chapter 9 discusses Sei Shōnagon's characteristic vocabulary.

TOPICS FOR DISCUSSION

1. The personality of Sei Shōnagon.
2. Why should a work seemingly frivolous in tone be considered one of the masterpieces of Japanese literature?
3. Sei Shōnagon's style and its importance in her work.
4. The Heian court as depicted in *The Pillow-Book.* Contrast with the world depicted in *The Tale of Genji.*
5. Sei Shōnagon's judgment on her society. The place of religion in her life.
6. The wit of Sei Shōnagon. Would *The Pillow-Book* bear out Meredith's opinion (in *Essay on Comedy*) that wit can exist only in a society in which men and women associate as equals?
7. The function of the lists in *The Pillow-Book.*

THE TALE OF GENJI (GENJI MONOGATARI), BY MURASAKI SHIKIBU

A long novel written about 1010 dealing with Prince Genji and his successors at the Japanese court of the tenth century. Usually considered the supreme work of Japanese literature.

TRANSLATIONS

a. COMPLETE

Benl, Oscar. *Genji-Monogatari. Die Geschichte vom Prinzen Genji.* 2 vols., Zürich, Manesse Verlag, 1966.
An excellent translation into German, with an introduction and table of persons in the work.

Waley, Arthur. *The Tale of Genji.* 2 vols., Boston, Houghton Mifflin, 1935; London, Allen and Unwin, 1935; 1 vol. ed., Boston, Houghton Mifflin, 1939; New York, Random House (Modern Library), 1960.
A superb rendering which captures beautifully the spirit of the original.

b. SELECTIONS

Haguenauer, Charles. *Le Genji Monogatari.* Paris, Presses Universitaires, 1959.
A fanatically literal version of Book I.

Suyematz, Kenchio. *Genji Monogatari.* London, Trübner, 1882; 2d ed. rev., Yokohama, Maruya, 1898.
A plodding, old-fashioned translation of about one third of the original. Affords an interesting comparison with Waley's version.

SECONDARY READINGS

Keene, Donald. "The Tale of Genji," in Wm. Theodore de
    Bary, ed., *Approaches to the Oriental Classics.* New York,
    Columbia University Press, 1959; pp. 186-95.
McCullough, William H. "Japanese Marriage Institutions in
    the Heian Period," *Harvard Journal of Asiatic Studies,*
    XXVII (1967), 103-67.
    A valuable study of the varieties of marriage institutions
    described in *The Tale of Genji* and other works of the period.
Morris, Ivan. *The World of the Shining Prince: Court Life in
    Ancient Japan.* Oxford University Press, 1964.
Omori, Annie S., and Kochi Doi. *Diaries of Court Ladies of
    Old Japan.* Boston and New York, Houghton Mifflin, 1920;
    London, Constable, 1921; 2d ed., Tokyo, Maruzen, 1935.
    Contains a pedestrian but useful translation of the diary of
    Murasaki Shikibu.
Sansom, Sir George B. *A History of Japan to 1334.* Stanford
    University Press, 1958; London, Cresset Press, 1959.
    Chapter 8 supplies the historical background of *The Tale of
    Genji;* Chapter 9, "The Rule of Taste," is an invaluable
    appreciation of it.
Tsunoda Ryusaku, Wm. Theodore de Bary, and Donald
    Keene, eds. *Sources of Japanese Tradition.* New York,
    Columbia University Press, 1958; paperback ed., 2 vols.,
    1964.
    Chapter 9 discusses the characteristic vocabulary of Mura-
    saki Shikibu and her contemporaries. Chapter 22 gives
    Motoori's memorable interpretation of *The Tale of Genji.*

TOPICS FOR DISCUSSION

1. *The Tale of Genji:* the first novel written anywhere in the
   world. How it differs from earlier adventure stories and
   romances. Its peculiar appeal to modern readers.
2. The world portrayed in the work: the court society. How
   its use of leisure differed from that of other court

societies. The cult of beauty. The cult of love. Reasons for indifference to social conditions.

3. The characters. What makes Prince Genji so appealing? Sensitivity as the touchstone in relations. The individuality of other characters.

4. The purpose of the novel. Murasaki's own views. Motoori's interpretation. Other theories.

5. Structure of the novel. Shift in tone as it progresses. Differences in the world before and after Genji's death.

6. Religious themes in the novel.

POETRY, FICTION, AND DIARIES OF THE NINTH TO ELEVENTH CENTURIES

Translations

a. COMPLETE

Bonneau, Georges. *Le monument poétique de Heian.* Paris, Geuthner, 1933-34.

Translation into French of a generous sampling from the *Kokinshū*, the great anthology of *waka* poetry of the period.

Cranston, Edwin A. *The Izumi Shikibu Diary.* Cambridge, Harvard University Press, 1969.

A good translation with an extensive introduction and notes.

Keene, Donald. "The Tale of the Bamboo Cutter," *Monumenta Nipponica*, XI (1956), 1-27.

McCullough, Helen Craig. *Tales of Ise.* Stanford, Stanford University Press, 1968.

A fluent translation with an excellent introduction.

Miner, Earl. *Japanese Poetic Diaries.* Los Angeles, University of California Press, 1969.

Includes a complete translation of the *Tosa Diary*.

Morris, Ivan. *As I Crossed a Bridge of Dreams.* New York, Dial Press, 1971.

A beautiful translation, with introduction, of *Sarashina Nikki*.

Omori, Annie S. and Kochi Doi. *Diaries of Court Ladies of Old Japan.* Boston, Houghton Mifflin, 1920; repr. Tokyo, Kenkyusha, 1935.

Poor translations of the *Izumi Shikibu Diary*, the *Murasaki Shikibu Diary* and the *Sarashina Diary*.

Vos, Frits. *A Study of the Ise-Monogatari with the Text According to the Den-Taika-Hippon.* 2 vols., The Hague, Mouton, 1957.
Includes a complete translation of *Tales of Ise* in a painstakingly literal style.

Whitehouse, Wilfred. *Ochikubo Monogatari.* London, Kegan Paul, Trench, Trubner, 1935; rev. ed., Tokyo, Hokuseido, 1965.
An uninspired translation of a Cinderella story.

b. SELECTIONS

Bownas, Geoffrey and Anthony Thwaite. *The Penguin Book of Japanese Verse.* Baltimore, Penguin Books, 1964.
Includes examples of *Kokinshū* poetry.

Cranston, Edwin A. "Atemiya, a Translation from the *Utsubo Monogatari,*" *Monumenta Nipponica,* XXIV (1969), 290-314.

Keene, Donald. *Anthology of Japanese Literature from the Earliest Era to the Mid-nineteenth Century.* New York, Grove Press (clothbound and paperback eds.), 1955.
Includes poetry and prose of the ninth and tenth centuries.

SECONDARY READINGS

Brower, Robert H. and Earl Miner. *Japanese Court Poetry.* Stanford, Stanford University Press, 1961.
Chapter V, "The Early Classical Period," is an analysis of the poetry of the *Kokinshū,* and includes translations of many examples.

Ueda Makoto. *Literary and Art Theories in Japan.* Cleveland, The Press of Case Western Reserve University, 1967.
Contains a chapter on Ki no Tsurayuki and his theories of poetry.

TOPICS FOR DISCUSSION

1. The formation of a Japanese poetic in the *Kokinshū*. What were the occasions recognized as appropriate for composing poetry? How do they differ from occasions chosen by *Manyōshū* poets?
2. The *tanka* as the classic Japanese verse form. What were some of the advantages and disadvantages of composing poetry in so brief a form? How did the choice of this form affect content?
3. The importance of the seasons in Japanese poetry.
4. The "poem tale" as a literary genre. Is the emphasis greater on the poetry or on the prose in *Tales of Ise*? In *Utsubo Monogatari*? The realism of the prose sections. Correlations between prose and poetry.
5. The fantastic story as a forerunner of serious prose. What is the level of literary sophistication in *The Tale of the Bamboo Cutter*? In the early sections of *Utsubo Monogatari*?
6. The diary as an important literary genre. The borderline between truth and fiction in the writing of literary diaries. The transition from the diary to the novel. The private diary and the public diary. Diaries by men and by women.
7. Buddhism and literature.

LITERATURE IN THE TWELFTH AND THIRTEENTH CENTURIES

TRANSLATIONS

Brower, Robert H. and Earl Miner. *Fujiwara Teika's Superior Poems of Our Time.* Stanford, Stanford University Press, 1967.

Translation of a collection edited by the great poet and critic Fujiwara Teika, together with an introduction.

Kato, Hilda. "The *Mumyōshō* of Kamo no Chōmei and Its Significance in Japanese Literature," *Monumenta Nipponica*, XXIII, no. 3-4 (1968), 321-430.

Translation of an extremely important collection of short essays on the art of Japanese poetry.

Keene, Donald. *Anthology of Japanese Literature from the Earliest Era to the Mid-nineteenth Century.* New York, Grove Press (clothbound and paperback eds.), 1955.

Includes translations of *An Account of My Hut (Hōjōki), The Lady Who Loved Insects (Mushi Mezuru Hime),* stories from the *Uji Shūi Monogatari,* and poetry from the *Shinkokinshū.*

Reischauer, Edwin O., and Joseph K. Yamagiwa. *Translations from Early Japanese Literature.* Cambridge, Harvard University Press, 1951.

Includes translations of the *Izayoi Diary,* the *Tsutsumi Chūnagon Monogatari,* and the *Heiji Monogatari.* The translations are literal.

Sadler, Arthur Lindsay. "*Heike Monogatari,*" *Transactions of the Asiatic Society of Japan,* 1st Ser. XLVI (1918) and XLIX (1921.).

A complete translation of one of the masterpieces of

Japanese literature, unfortunately in a rather ponderous style.

Yamagiwa, Joseph K. *The Ōkagami.* London, Allen and Unwin, 1967.

A complete, excessively literal translation of an important historical tale.

SECONDARY READINGS

Brower, Robert H. "Ex-Emperor Go-Toba's Secret Teachings," *Harvard Journal of Asiatic Studies,* XXXII (1972), 5-70.

Brower, Robert H., and Earl Miner. *Japanese Court Poetry.* Stanford, Stanford University Press, 1961.

Chapter VI, "The Mid-Classical Period," is devoted mainly to the *Shinkokinshū*, analyzed with many translations.

Butler, Kenneth Dean. "The Textual Evolution of the *Heike Monogatari,*" *Harvard Journal of Asiatic Studies,* XXVI (1966), 5-51.

Konishi Jin'ichi. "Association and Progression: Principles of Integration in Anthologies of Japanese Court Poetry, A.D. 900–1350," *Harvard Journal of Asiatic Studies,* XXI (1958), 67-127.

An important essay translated and adapted from the Japanese by Robert H. Brower and Earl Miner. Deals chiefly with the *Shinkokinshū*.

Sansom, Sir George B. *A History of Japan to 1334.* Stanford, Stanford University Press, 1958; repr. London, Cresset Press, 1959.

Chapter 14, "The Gempei War," describes the military and political events that formed the background for much of the literature of this period.

Tsunoda Ryusaku, Wm. Theodore de Bary, and Donald Keene. *Sources of Japanese Tradition.* New York, Columbia University Press, 1958; paperback ed., 2 vols., 1964.

Chapter 10, "Amida and the Pure Land," deals with the variety of Buddhism most characteristic of this period.

TOPICS FOR DISCUSSION

1. Discuss the change in tone between the Heian masterpieces and those of the Kamakura period. What historical events help to explain it?
2. How strong is the influence of Amida Buddhism in *Account of My Hut*? Could a similar work have been written without Buddhist influence?
3. The personality of Kamo no Chōmei as revealed in *Account of My Hut* and in *Mumyōshō*.
4. Does the criticism found in *Mumyōshō* have a wider application than the analysis of how to write a successful *waka*? The "modernity" of Chōmei's views. Does "symbolism" seem an appropriate term for the kind of poetry he advocated?
5. What disasters are omitted from Kamo no Chōmei's enumeration in *Account of My Hut*? What reasons might have dictated this silence?
6. The attitude toward warfare displayed in *Heiji Monogatari* and in *Heike Monogatari*. Are these works celebrations of victories or commemorations of defeats? Is the tone epic?
7. Structure of *Heike Monogatari*. Can it be considered as a novel? The claims of history versus the claims of literature. Why should *Heike Monogatari* have provided the materials for innumerable works of the theater?
8. Fujiwara Teika, the arbiter of poetic taste. His poetic views. The manner of compiling and arranging an anthology. The *Shinkokinshū*, a distinctively different kind of collection from the *Kokinshū*.
9. Historical fiction and fictionalized history. How does *Ōkagami* compare with *Heike Monogatari* as an historical work? As a work of literature?

TSUREZURE-GUSA, BY YOSHIDA KENKŌ

Essays of varying lengths written about 1330 by a worldly priest.

TRANSLATIONS

Benl, Oscar. *Tsurezuregusa oder Aufzeignungen aus Musse-stunden.* Tokyo, Kultur-Institut, 1940; Bergen, Müller und Kiepenheuer, 1948.

Keene, Donald. *Essays in Idleness.* New York, Columbia University Press, 1967.
A complete translation with an introduction.

Kurata Ryukichi. *The Harvest of Leisure, Translated from the Tsure-zure Gusa.* (Wisdom of the East series.) London, John Murray, 1931.
An unsatisfactory translation.

Sansom, Sir George B. "The Tsuredzure Gusa of Yoshida no Kaneyoshi," *Transactions of the Asiatic Society of Japan,* XXXIX (1911), 231-41.
A nearly complete translation into readable English. Excerpts are included in Donald Keene's *Anthology of Japanese Literature from the Earliest Era to the Mid-nineteenth Century* (New York, Grove Press, 1955) under the title *Essays in Idleness.*

SECONDARY READINGS

Sansom, Sir George B. *Japan, A Short Cultural History.* London, Cresset Press, 1931; New York, Century, 1931;

rev. ed., New York, Appleton Century Crofts, 1943; London, Cresset Press, 1946.

Chapter 18 treats Kenkō's time.

Tsunoda Ryusaku, Wm. Theodore de Bary, and Donald Keene, eds. *Sources of Japanese Tradition.* New York, Columbia University Press, 1958; paperback ed., 2 vols., 1964.

Chapter 14 discusses some of the aesthetic concepts of the *Tsurezure-gusa.*

TOPICS FOR DISCUSSION

1. Why should this book have become one of the most popular of all Japanese literary works?
2. What resemblances and points of difference are there between *The Pillow-Book* and *Tsurezure-gusa?*
3. Kenkō as an arbiter of Japanese taste. His views on houses, interior decoration, gardens, tradition in art.
4. Kenkō as an arbiter of Japanese manners. The behavior of the gentleman and of the boor.
5. Aesthetic theories. Beginning and End. The importance of the perishability of beauty.
6. Kenkō's personality. His friends.
.7. Kenkō's concerns—this worldly or other-worldly?

THE NŌ PLAYS

*Short plays in a mixture of poetry and prose, written chiefly in
the fourteenth and fifteenth centuries.*

TRANSLATIONS

Keene, Donald, ed. *Twenty Plays of the Nō Theatre.* Columbia
University Press, 1970; paperback ed. also.
Most of the plays have not been previously translated.
Introductions, stage directions and figures in the text help to
clarify the presentation.
Nippon Gakujutsu Shinkōkai. *Japanese Noh Drama.* Vols. 1
and 2. Tokyo, Nippon Gakujutsu Shinkōkai, 1955, 1959.
Vol. 3 (*The Noh Drama*). Tokyo and Rutland, Vt., Tuttle,
1960.
Translations of 30 plays with valuable introductions. Figures
in the text are helpful in suggesting the movements of the
actors. The language of the translations is somewhat old-
fashioned.
Peri, Noël. *Le Nô.* Tokyo, Maison Franco-Japonaise, 1944.
Ten Nō plays and eleven *kyōgen* with valuable introductory
material.
Ueda Makoto. *The Old Pine Tree and Other Noh Plays.*
Lincoln, University of Nebraska Press, 1962.
A program of five plays well translated with a good
introduction.
Waley, Arthur. *The Nō Plays of Japan.* London, Allen and
Unwin, 1921; New York, Knopf, 1922; New York, Grove
Press (Evergreen), 1957.
Graceful renderings of 19 plays with summaries of others.

SECONDARY READINGS

Keene, Donald. *Japanese Literature: An Introduction for Western Readers*. London, John Murray, 1953; New York, Grove Press (Evergreen), 1955.
Contains a general discussion of the aesthetics of the Nō.
—— *Nō, the Classical Theatre of Japan*. Tokyo and Palo Alto, California, Kodansha International, 1966.
A discussion of the background of Nō theatre, the history and the presentation, illustrated with many photographs.
O'Neill, Patrick G. *Early Nō Drama, Its Background, Character and Development 1300-1450*. London, Lund Humphries, 1959.
A scholarly examination of the background, character, and development of the Nō.
Shidehara Michitarō, and Wilfred Whitehouse, trs. "Seami's Sixteen Treatises," *Monumenta Nipponica*, IV, no. 2 (1941), 204-39; V, no. 2 (1942), 180-214.
Sieffert, René. *La tradition secrète du Nô*. Paris, Gallimard, 1960.
An excellent translation of works of criticism by Zeami (Seami), together with the translation of a typical Nō program of plays.
Tsunoda Ryusaku, Wm. Theodore de Bary, and Donald Keene, eds. *Sources of Japanese Tradition*. New York, Columbia University Press, 1958; paperback ed., 2 vols., 1964.
Chapter 14 includes translations of representative works of criticism by Seami.
Ueda Makoto. *Zeami, Bashō, Yeats, Pound*. The Hague, Mouton, 1965.
The chapter on Zeami has the subtitle: "Imitation, *Yūgen*, and the Sublime."
Zeami. *Kadensho*. Tr. by Sakurai Chūichi, and others. Kyoto, Foundation of Sumiya-Shinobe Scholarship, 1968.

TOPICS FOR DISCUSSION

1. Physical resemblances of the Nō plays to Greek tragedy. In what ways do they contrast most sharply with Greek tragedy?
2. The structure and the language of the plays.
3. The functions of ghosts in the Nō plays.
4. Buddhist themes in the plays.
5. How can plays that give little or no attention to character development, conflict of characters, or even plot, manage nevertheless to move audiences?
6. What of the plays is lost when we read the text instead of seeing them?
7. How do stage conventions of Nō restrict the expression of dramatic ideas? How do they make possible types of expression not generally found in other theatres?

THE NOVELS OF IHARA SAIKAKU (1642–93)

Novels by the greatest of the novelists of the Tokugawa period, chiefly about love and money.

TRANSLATIONS

De Bary, Wm. Theodore. *Five Women Who Loved Love.* Tokyo and Rutland, Vt., Tuttle, 1956.
A complete translation into readable English of Saikaku's masterpiece, *Kōshoku gonin onna.*

Hamada Kengi. *The Life of an Amorous Man.* Tokyo and Rutland, Vt., Tuttle, 1963.
An excessively free translation of Saikaku's first novel, a work of interest to students of literary history but otherwise inferior.

Hibbett, Howard. *The Floating World in Japanese Fiction.* London, Oxford University Press, 1959.
Includes selections from *Kōshoku ichidai onna (The Woman Who Spent Her Life in Love).*

Morris, Ivan. *The Life of an Amorous Woman and Other Writings.* Norfolk, Conn., New Directions, 1963.
Selections from Saikaku's principal works, translated into an idiom reminiscent of Defoe.

Sargent, G. W. *The Japanese Family Storehouse (Nihon Eitaigura), or, The Millionaires' Gospel Modernised.* London, Cambridge University Press, 1959.
A complete translation of a collection of tales about merchants who made and lost fortunes.

Takatsuka Masanori and David C. Stubbs. *This Scheming World.* Tokyo and Rutland, Vt., Tuttle, 1965.

A good translation of one of Saikaku's last works, a series of short tales about the desperate stratagems men employ in order to pay their annual debts at New Year.

SECONDARY READINGS

Most of the above volumes of translations are equipped with excellent introductions and other explanatory material, which afford the best guide to Saikaku and his age.

Sansom, Sir George B. *Japan, A Short Cultural History.* London, Cresset Press, 1931; New York, Century, 1931; rev. ed., New York, Appleton Century Crofts, 1943; London, Cresset Press, 1946.
Chapter 22, "Genroku," gives the background of Saikaku's period.

TOPICS FOR DISCUSSION

1. The emergence of a major popular literature in Japan; contrast with the works previously read.
2. Saikaku as a master stylist.
3. Saikaku's attitude toward his characters—a mixture of detachment and affection.
4. Saikaku's attitude towards love. Contrast with *The Tale of Genji.*
5. Saikaku and money.
6. Saikaku's humor.
7. Saikaku's immorality.

THE POETRY AND PROSE OF MATSUO BASHŌ (1644–94)

Poetry and prose by the master of the haiku, *and one of the greatest of all Japanese poets.*

TRANSLATIONS

Corman, Cid, and Kamaike Susumu. *Back Roads to Far Towns: Bashō's Oku-no-Hosomichi.* New York, Grossman, 1968.
A translation into a jagged, modern English that attempts to suggest the elliptic qualities of the original text.

Henderson, Harold G. *An Introduction to Haiku: An Anthology of Poems and Poets from Bashō to Shiki.* New York, Doubleday, 1958.
Includes graceful translations of *haiku* by Bashō and his school.

Keene, Donald. *Anthology of Japanese Literature from the Earliest Era to the Mid-nineteenth Century.* New York, Grove Press, 1955.
Contains excerpts from *The Narrow Road of Oku* and other writings.

Miner, Earl. *Japanese Poetic Diaries.* Los Angeles, University of California Press, 1969.
Includes *Narrow Road through the Provinces (Oku no Hosomichi).*

Yuasa Nobuyuki. *The Narrow Road to the Deep North and Other Travel Sketches.* Baltimore, Penguin Books, 1966.
Complete translation of Bashō's five travel accounts, together with an introduction.

SECONDARY READINGS

Blyth, R. H. *Haiku*. 4 vols. Tokyo, Kamakura Bunko, 1949-52. Includes many *haiku* by Bashō with lengthy explanations.

Keene, Donald. "Bashō's Journey to Sarashina," *Transactions of the Asiatic Society of Japan*, December, 1957. A translation of one of Bashō's travel accounts, with a description of its importance.

——— "Bashō's Journey of 1684," *Asia Major* (new series), VII (1959), 131-44. Translation of Bashō's first travel account.

McKinnon, Richard N. "Tanka and Haiku: Some Aspects of Classical Japanese Poetry," in H. Frenz and G. L. Anderson, eds., *Indiana University Conference on Oriental-Western Literary Relations*. Chapel Hill, University of North Carolina Press, 1955; pp. 67-84.

Tsunoda Ryusaku, Wm. Theodore de Bary, and Donald Keene, eds. *Sources of Japanese Tradition*. New York, Columbia University Press, 1958; paperback ed., 2 vols., 1964. Chapter 20, "The Haiku and the Democracy of Poetry in Japan," includes translations of works by Bashō and a discussion of the *haiku* as a social phenomenon in Japan.

TOPICS FOR DISCUSSION

1. What makes a good *haiku*? What can a *haiku* do better than most other types of poetry? What can a *haiku* not do?
2. The eternal and the ever-changing in *haiku*: Bashō's insistence that the *haiku* must include both.
3. Immutability of language in the *haiku*.
4. Relation between Bashō's *haiku* and his prose.
5. Bashō's appreciation of Chinese literature.
6. Bashō and Japanese tradition   To what degree does his poetry reflect his own society?
7. The subjects treated by Bashō. Is it proper to speak of him as a "poet of Nature"?

THE PLAYS OF CHIKAMATSU MONZAEMON (1653-1725)

Works for the puppet stage, mainly concerned with the lives of the merchant class.

TRANSLATIONS

Keene, Donald. *Major Plays of Chikamatsu.* New York, Columbia University Press, 1961.

Eleven plays with an introduction. Four of these plays are also available under the title *Four Major Plays of Chikamatsu* (New York, Columbia University Press [paperback], 1964).

Miyamori Asataro. *Masterpieces of Chikamatsu, the Japanese Shakespeare.* London, Kegan Paul, Trench, Trubner, 1926; New York, Dutton, 1926.

An introduction and an old-fashioned, rather slipshod translation of six plays.

Shively, Donald H. *The Love Suicide at Amijima.* Cambridge, Harvard University Press, 1953.

A translation with extensive notes of one of Chikamatsu's most important plays.

SECONDARY READINGS

Bowers, Faubion. *Japanese Theatre.* New York, Hermitage House, 1952.

Includes a discussion of Chikamatsu's plays.

Dunn, C. J. *The Early Japanese Puppet Drama.* London, Luzac, 1966.

A scholarly examination of the history of the puppet theatre from its origins up to the time of Chikamatsu, including translations of some early plays.

Keene, Donald. *The Battles of Coxinga: Chikamatsu's Puppet Play, Its Background and Importance.* London, Taylor's Foreign Press, 1951.
Includes a history of the puppet theatre.

————*Bunraku, The Art of the Japanese Puppet Theatre.* Tokyo and Palo Alto, California, Kodansha International, 1965.
A study òf all aspects of the puppet theatre, illustrated with many excellent photographs.

Tsunoda Ryusaku, Wm. Theodore de Bary, and Donald Keene, eds. *Sources of Japanese Tradition.* New York, Columbia University Press, 1958; paperback ed., 2 vols., 1964.
See especially chapter 19, "The Vocabulary of Japanese Aesthetics, III."

TOPICS FOR DISCUSSION

1. The characteristics of the Japanese popular theatre: how Chikamatsu's dramas differ from Nō in intent and audience; how Chikamatsu's dramas differ from Shakespeare's in characters and subjects.
2. Is it proper to speak of Chikamatsu's dramas as tragedies? What might Aristotle have said about them? What gives the characters their stature? To what degree do they determine their own fates?
3. The function of the narrator in creating dramatic situation and character.
4. The conflict between love and duty found in the plays.
5. Differing attitudes of Chikamatsu and Saikaku towards their characters.
6. Chikamatsu's special concessions to the requirements of the puppet stage.
7. Chikamatsu's plays as a mirror of their time.

CHŪSHINGURA (*ca.* 1748), BY TAKEDA IZUMO, MIYOSHI SHŌRAKU, AND NAMIKI SENRYŪ

The most popular of all Japanese plays. Originally written for the puppet stage, but now best known in Kabuki productions.

TRANSLATIONS

Inouye Jukichi. *Chūshingura, or, Forty Seven Ronin.* 4th rev. ed. Tokyo, Maruzan, 1937.
Complete translation with an introduction (revision of *Chūsingura, or, The Treasury of Loyal Retainers* [Tokyo, Nakanishi-ya, 1910]). The English is old-fashioned and rather stilted.
Keene, Donald. *Chūshingura: The Treasury of Loyal Retainers.* New York, Columbia University Press, 1971.

SECONDARY READINGS

Richie, Donald, and Miyoko Watanabe. *Six Kabuki Plays.* Tokyo, Hokuseido Press, 1963.
Includes extract translation of four scenes of *Chūshingura*.
Sansom, Sir George B. *Japan, A Short Cultural History.* London, Cresset Press, 1931; New York, Century, 1931; rev. ed., New York, Appleton Century Crofts, 1943; London, Cresset Press, 1946.
Chapter 23, "The Breakdown of Feudalism," interprets eighteenth-century Japan.
Shioya Sakae. *Chūshingura: An Exposition.* Tokyo, Hokuseido Press, 1940.
A popularized version of the historical background, together with a summary of the play.

Topics for Discussion

1. Reasons for the immense popularity of this play with all classes of Japanese.
2. The feudal morality of the play. Why were its ideals so absorbing to audiences in eighteenth-century Japan? Why should they still be absorbing today, when the feudal morality has been rejected?
3. Characters in the play. Are they believable as individuals or do they tend to be types? Comparison with characters in Chikamatsu's plays. The variety of persons in the play.
4. Violence and delicacy—characteristic aspects of Japanese life found in this play. How are they resolved?
5. Dramatic structure of *Chūshingura*.

LITERATURE OF THE MEIJI PERIOD (1868–1912)

TRANSLATIONS

Fukuzawa Yukichi. *The Autobiography of Yukichi Fukuzawa.* Revised translation by Eiichi Kiyooka. New York, Columbia University Press, 1966.
Futabatei Shimei. *Ukigumo.* Tr. by Marleigh Grayer Ryan in *Japan's First Modern Novel: Ukigumo.* New York, Columbia University Press, 1967.
A complete translation with an extensive introduction.
Ishikawa Takuboku. *Poems to Eat.* Tr. by Carl Sesar. Tokyo and Palo Alto, California, Kodansha International, 1966.
Keene, Donald, ed. *Modern Japanese Literature, An Anthology.* New York, Grove Press (clothbound and paperback eds.), 1956.
Includes selections from the poetry, fiction, drama, and diaries of the period.
Mori Ōgai. *The Wild Geese.* Tr. by Sanford Goldstein and Kaigo Ochiai. Tokyo, Tuttle, 1959.
Natsume Sōseki. *Botchan.* Tr. by Alan Turney. Tokyo and Palo Alto, California, Kodansha International, 1972.
—— *Grass on the Wayside.* Tr. by Edwin McClellan. Chicago, University of Chicago Press, 1969.
—— *I Am a Cat.* Tr. by Katsue Shibata and Motonari Kai. Tokyo, Kenkyusha, 1961.
—— *Kokoro.* Tr. by Edwin McClellan. Chicago, Henry Regnery (paperback), 1967.
—— *Mon* (The Gate). Tr. by Francis Mathy. London, Peter Owen, 1972.
—— *The Three-Cornered World.* Tr. by Alan Turney. London, Peter Owen, 1965; repr. Chicago, Henry Regnery, 1967.

—— *The Wayfarer*. Tr. by Beongcheon Yu. Detroit, Wayne State University Press, 1967.

SECONDARY READINGS

Blacker, Carmen. *The Japanese Enlightenment: A Study of the Writings of Fukuzawa Yukichi*. New York, Cambridge University Press, 1964.
Henderson, Harold G. *An Introduction to Haiku*. New York, Doubleday Anchor (paperback), 1958.
Contains one chapter on Masaoka Shiki (1867-1902), the most famous *haiku* poet of the Meiji period.
Keene, Donald. *Modern Japanese Novels and the West*. Charlottesville, University of Virginia Press, 1961.
An essay on the creation of modern Japanese fiction.
—— *Modern Japanese Poetry: An Essay*. Ann Arbor, University of Michigan Press, 1964.
Kono Ichirō, and Rikutarō Fukuda. *An Anthology of Modern Japanese Poetry*. Tokyo, Kenkyusha, 1957.
McClellan, Edwin. *Two Japanese Novelists: Sōseki and Tōson*. Chicago, University of Chicago Press, 1969.
McKinnon, Richard N. *The Heart is Alone: A Selection of 20th Century Japanese Short Stories*. Tokyo, Hokuseido, 1957.
Morris, Ivan. *Modern Japanese Stories*. London, Eyre and Spottiswoode, 1961; repr. Tokyo and Rutland, Vermont, Tuttle, 1962.
Okazaki Yoshie. *Japanese Literature in the Meiji Era*. Tr. and adapted by V. H. Viglielmo. Tokyo, Ōbunsha, 1955.
An extremely detailed work, useful for reference rather than as an introduction to the literature of the period.
Seidensticker, Edward. *Kafū the Scribbler: The Life and Writings of Nagai Kafū, 1879-1959*. Stanford, Stanford University Press, 1965; paperback ed. also.
Includes translations of fiction by a writer whose early works were composed during the Meiji period.

TOPICS FOR DISCUSSION

1. In what ways do the writings of the early Meiji period most immediately reveal Western influence?
2. What elements in Japanese writing proved most resistant to Western influence?
3. Fukuzawa Yukichi as an archetypal figure of the Meiji period. Trace his shifting attitudes toward the West and toward the traditional Japanese virtues.
4. Imagery in the Meiji period as contrasted with imagery in traditional Japanese poetry. Content, form, and language of Meiji poetry.
5. Why should symbolism have appealed so greatly to modern Japanese poets?
6. Takuboku's reasons for using the classical verse form, the *tanka,* to express completely untraditional thoughts. Do his longer poems suggest he made a wise choice in preferring the *tanka?*
7. The achievement of Futabatei Shimei in creating a modern Japanese novel. What are his indebtednesses to the Japanese past? To Russian literature? What was uniquely his own? Did he sympathize with or condemn Bunzō?
8. Why did Natsume Sōseki become the most popular and esteemed Japanese novelist of modern times? The varieties of his work. His humor and his gloom. His indebtedness to English fiction and thought. His views on traditional Japanese aesthetics and morality. Inarticulateness as a factor in his novels.
9. The "I novel" in Meiji Japan. Discuss the autobiographical fiction of Natsume Sōseki, Mori Ōgai, and Shimazaki Tōson.

Companions To Asian Studies

Introduction To Oriental Civilizations

Wm. Theodore de Bary, *Editor*

Sources of Japanese Tradition 1958 Paperback ed., 2 vols. 1964

Sources of Indian Tradition 1958 Paperback ed., 2 vols. 1964

Sources of Chinese Tradition 1960 Paperback ed., 2 vols. 1964

Translations From The Oriental Classics

Major Plays of Chikamatsu, tr. Donald Keene 1961

Records of the Grand Historian of China, translated from the Shih chi of Ssu-ma Ch'ien, tr. Burton Watson, 2 vols. 1961

Instructions for Practical Living and Other Neo-Confucian Writings by Wang Yang-ming, tr. Wing-tsit Chan 1963

Chuang Tzu: Basic Writings, tr. Burton Watson, paperback ed. only 1964

The Mahābhārata, tr. Chakravarthi V. Narasimhan 1965

The Manyōshū, Nippon Gakujutsu Shinkōkai edition 1965

Su Tung-p'o: Selections from a Sung Dynasty Poet, tr. Burton Watson 1965

Bhartrihari: Poems, tr. Barbara Stoler Miller. Also in paperback ed. 1967

Basic Writings of Mo Tzu, Hsün Tzu, and Han Fei Tzu, tr. Burton Watson. Also in separate paperback eds. 1967

The Awakening of Faith, attributed to Aśvaghosha, tr. Yoshito S. Hakeda 1967

Reflections on Things at Hand: The Neo-Confucian Anthology, comp. Chu Hsi and Lü Tsu-ch'ien, tr. Wing-tsit Chan 1967

Studies In Oriental Culture